NORTH CAROLINA SLAVES
AND
FREE PERSONS OF COLOR

CHOWAN COUNTY

VOLUME ONE

William L. Byrd, III

HERITAGE BOOKS
2019

HERITAGE BOOKS
AN IMPRINT OF HERITAGE BOOKS, INC.

Books, CDs, and more—Worldwide

For our listing of thousands of titles see our website at
www.HeritageBooks.com

Published 2019 by
HERITAGE BOOKS, INC.
Publishing Division
5810 Ruatan Street
Berwyn Heights, Md. 20740

Copyright © 2002 William L. Byrd, III

All rights reserved. No part of this book may be reproduced or transmitted in any form or by any means, electronic or mechanical, including photocopying, recording or by any information storage and retrieval system without written permission from the author, except for the inclusion of brief quotations in a review.

International Standard Book Number
Paperbound: 978-0-7884-2182-2

Contents

Introduction	*vii*
Acknowledgements	*ix*
Chapter One	***1***
Chowan County	1
Magistrates Court Records	1
Chapter Two	***11***
Chowan County	11
Civil Actions	11
Chapter Three	***23***
Chowan County	23
Criminal Actions	23
Chapter Four	***33***
Chowan County	33
Gun Permits	33
Chapter Five	***39***
Chowan County	39
Patrol Records	39
Chapter Six	***151***
Chowan County	151
Bills of Sale	151
Chapter Seven	***159***
Chowan County	159
Free Persons of Color	159
Chapter Eight	***163***

Chowan County _____ 163
    Hiring of Slaves _____ 163

Chapter Nine _____ *167*
    Chowan County _____ 167
    Division of Slaves _____ 167

Chapter Ten _____ *187*
    Chowan County _____ 187
    Miscellaneous Records _____ 187

Appendix A _____ *197*
Glossary of Legal Terms _____ *197*
Table of Cases _____ *199*
    Civil and Criminal Actions _____ 199
Index _____ *201*

Introduction

The records in this book were transcribed from original papers located in the North Carolina State Archives. Most of these papers are listed under general headings such as "Slaves and Free Negroes, " or "Slaves and Free Persons of Color." Occasionally they are listed under the heading of "Miscellaneous Records."[1]

This particular group of papers were selected from the North Carolina county of Chowan. Not a few of these records are torn and faded. In some cases, part of the original text is missing, and many of the names of individuals are almost indecipherable. Nevertheless, every attempt has been made to transcribe these papers as accurately as possible.

Included are a plethora of civil and criminal actions pertaining to slaves and free persons of color. The interactions between both Blacks and Whites are displayed on an antagonistic and intimate level, and are dramatically played out through crime and punishment. The criminal cases are filled with intrigue involving murder, felonies, trading with slaves and harboring slaves.

The different sections of this book are broken down into the following categories: Magistrates Court Records, Civil Actions, Criminal

---

[1] Thornton W. Mitchell, "Preliminary Guide to Records Relating to Blacks in the North Carolina State Archives," *Archives Information Circular* 17(June 1980): 3-4.

Actions, Gun Permits, Patrol Records, Bills of Sale, Free Persons of Color, Hiring of Slaves, Division of Slaves, and Miscellaneous Records.

There was a large packet of Slave Patrol Records included with these papers, generating hundreds of names from the different Patrol Districts. Slave owners generally served as Patrol Officers for one year.

Chowan County was formed in 1670. It began as a precinct in Albemarle County. It was named in honor of the Chowan Indians, who lived in the northeastern part of the Colony. Chowan County is bounded by Albemarle Sound, Chowan River, and Bertie, Hertford, Gates, and Perquimans counties. The county seat, Edenton, was established in 1720, and has continued to be the county seat since that time. Part of Tyrell, Hertford and Gates were formed from Chowan.[2]

---

[2] David Leroy Corbitt, *The Formation of the North Carolina Counties: 1663-1943* (Raleigh: Division of Archives and History, 1950) 65-66

Acknowledgements

The Publishing of this book would not have been possible without the valuable help and assistance of the staff of the North Carolina State Archives.

Chowan County
Magistrates Courts Records

Chapter One

Chowan County

Magistrates Court Records

North Carolina State Archives
Chowan County Records
Miscellaneous Slave Records
C.R.024.928.3

Dom Rex Vs. Yorkshire, a Slave
Felony, Stealing
Chowan County [Date not given.]

North Carolina }
Chowan County }

Chowan County
Magistrates Courts Records

Pursuant to a Warrant from Joseph Blount Esquire directed to the Sheriff of this County aforesaid requiring him to Summon three of his Majesty's Justices and four freeholders and owners of Slaves pursuant to an Act of Assembly for Triall of Slaves. The Sheriff Returned the following persons To Witt

Joseph Blount, Edward Vail & James Luten, Esquires & Justices

William Hoskins, Henderson Standing, Malachi Wo[?], & John Charlton, Freeholders & Owners of Slaves

Who met According and Qualified According to Law Whereas a Negroe fellow Named Yorkshire of the property of Penelope Craven Wido. Being Convicted by his own Confession of Stealing a parcell of Deer Skins of the property of Mr. Robert Nelson in Trust for Mr. William Lowther, Ordered that this Said Yorkshire be Carried to the Wipping post and receive One hundred Lashes Well laid on his bare back and afterwards have his Ears Nailed to the Whipping post and Cutt off and Bob a Negroe fellow of the property of Mrs. Cravon Afsd. Ordered that he be Carried to the Whipping post aforesaid and receive One hundred Lashes well laid on his bare back and afterwards to have his Ears Nailed to the post & Cutt Off, and that Mingo a Negroe fellow the property of James Thompson On his giving false Evidences it is Ordered that he receive Sixty Lashes at the Whipping post aforesaid and to have One Ear Nailed to the post and Cut Off.

Jos. Blount, Edw Vail, Willm. Hoskins, Hen'd Standin, Malachi Wo[?], John Charlton

****

Dom Rex Vs Moses, a Slave
Felony
Chowan County [1757]

North Carolina,
    At a Special Court held at the Court House in Edenton in the County of Chowan in the year of our Lord one thousand Seven hundred and fifty Seven for the Summary Tryall of Negroe Moses by virtue of an

Chowan County
Magistrates Courts Records

Act of Assembly of the Province aforesaid Entitled an Act for Tryall of Slaves Committing offences Crimes and Misdeameanors.

Present the Worshipfull Edward Fail, William Hoskins, & Robert Lenox, Esquires Justices

William Luten Jr., Cornelias Leary, John Luten & James Haughton, Freeholders and owners of Negroes

Joseph Blount Esquire, Sheriff

      The Court met and Qualified According to law and proceeded regularly to this Tryall of the Negroe Slave Moses aforementioned. And upon his Arraignment he plead not Guilty.
      The Court upon Consideration find the aforesaid Negroe Moses the Property of John Campbell Esquire Guilty of the felony said to his Charge and do order the said Negroe Moses to be hanged by Joseph Blount Esquire High Sheriff of this County Between the Hours of five and six O'Clock this present Evening being the Twenty Second of this Instant August in the year of our Lord One thousand Seven hundred and fifty seven at the Gallows in this Town of Edenton. The Court then proceeded to Valuation of the aforesaid Negroe Slave, and Valued him in this sum of Sixty Pounds proclamation Money to be paid the Publick.

The foregoing Orders were Read and Signed by the Following Gentlemens. Edw Fail, William Hoskins, Ro Lenox, Wm. Luten, Cornelias Leary, Jn. Luten & Jas. Houghton - Order [?] [?]

****

State Vs Sam, a Slave
Felony, Attempted Murder
Chowan County [1781]

The Tryal of Negro Sam

Edenton SS
      Whereas complaint hath this day been made to me by Michael Payne Esqr. that a certain Negroe called Sam, a Slave of William Savage Esqr. Committed a Violent Breach of the peace in his Kitchen on the

Chowan County
Magistrates Courts Records

Twenty sixth day of Decr. Last past by attempting to put to Death a certain Negroe called Ishmael now in the service of William Bennet Esqr. putting in Terror & affright his Family against the peace of the State.

These are therefore in the name of the State to summon three Justices of the Peace and four Freeholders, owners of Slaves of the County of Chowan to be & appear at the Court House at Eleven oClock in the forenoon on the tenth day of this Instant to Hear, Judge & award Judgment on the above Complaint for so doing this is your Warrant Given under my hand & Seal this 8th day of Jany. 1781
To

John Hartford, Constable
Rob Smith   (Seal)

Summons Saml & Arch Bell & Dominique Pambrie[?] to be & appear According to the time of the within written Warrant to testify in this Behalf & also warn Squire Barker, Joe, Mr.Grays London, M Paynes Thamer & Kate, Mrs. Cheshires Ishmael
Ro Smith

State of North Carolina }
Chowan County   }

The Tryal of Negro Sam the Property of William Savage for attempting to Kill a Negro Fellow by the name of Ishmael now in the Service of William Bennett Esqr. January 9th 1781.

Present the Worshipfull Justices William Boyd, Robert Hardy & Cha. Johnson. Freeholders, Joseph Blount, John Poynter, Robert Egan, David Lawrence.

Ordered that the Constable take the said Negro Sam to the Whiping Post and there give him One hundred Lashes and then to be Committed to the Goal and there to Remain till his Master gives Security in Bond of Forty Thousand Pounds that he doth no Mischief with Fire Arms for the future, Given under our hands & Seals the day & year above mentioned.
Wm Boyd   (Seal)
Rob Hardy   (Seal)

Chowan County
Magistrates Courts Records

Chas. Johnson   (Seal)
John Poynter   (Seal)
Jos Blount   (Seal)
David Lawrence   (Seal)
Robt Egan   (Seal)

****

State Vs. Jim, a Slave
Felony
Chowan County [1781]

State of North Carolina }
Chowan County }

At a Court begun & held at Edenton this twenty first Day of July one thousand Seven hundred & eighty one, for the Tryal of a Negro Man Jim, now the Property, and Slave of Major Josiah Copeland for having in his possession a Quantity of Powder, Shott & Sugar contrary to Law.

Present, John Baptist Beasley, Charles Bonfield, & Thomas White, Esquires & Justices.

William Hoskins, Jacob Simons, Lemuel Creecy & Jonathan Boulton, Gentlemen Freeholders.

The Court Hearing the Testimony against the Prisoner Order he shall be Carried to the Publick Whiping Post & there receive one hundred stripes well laid on his bare Back & then Discharged, his Owner to pay all Costs.
Jn B Beasley, Chas Bondfield, Thos White, Willm. Hoskins, Leml Creecy, Jacob Simons & Jonathan Boulton

****

State Vs. Jacob, a Slave
Murder
Chowan County [1787]

Chowan County
Magistrates Courts Records

At a Court Called & held at the Court House in Edenton on the fifteenth day of October 1787 for the Tryal of Negro John the property of Samuel Johnston Esquire Charged with the Murder of a Negro Call'd Sandy the property of Mr Josiah Collins

Present, Michael Payne, Stephen Cabarrus & Nathaniel Allen, Esquires & Justices

William Littlejohn, Samuel Butler, Alexander Black & Thomas King, Gentlemen, Freeholders & Owners of Salves.

The Prisoner brought into Court & Arraigned at the Bar pleads Not Guilty & puts himself upon this Worshipfull Court for his Tryal. The Court after hearing the evidence and maturely weighing the circumstances say the Prisoner is guilty of the Murder as charged in the Warrant, and is to be carried to the Common Gallows on Thursday next and there to be hung by the Neck between the hours of Eleven & one o'Clock in the afternoon untill he is dead
Michl. Payne, S.Cabarrus, Nathl. Allen, Wm. Littlejohn, Saml Butler, Alexr. Black & Thomas King

****

State Vs. Jacob, a Slave
Felony, Stealing
Chowan County [1789]

Trial of Negro Jacob
The property of the Estate of Willm. Hoskins Decd.
22 Jany. 1789

Chowan County
To the Sheriff of said County, Greetings:
    You are hereby ordered to Summon three Justices & four Freeholders to Meet at the Court House at two oClock this afternoon, to sitt as a Court for the Trial of Negro Jacob the property of the Estate of William Hoskins deceas'd for Stealing one Hogg the property of John Blount, and for so doing this shall be your Sufficient Authority. Given under my Hands & Seal this 22nd day of January 1789
Michl. Payne

Chowan County
Magistrates Courts Records

At a Court Called and held at the Court House in Edenton on Thursday the 22nd Jany. 1789 for the Trial of Negro Jacob the property of the Estate of William Hoskins Deceas'd for Stealing one hog the property of John Blount

Present, Thomas Benbury, Michl. Payne, William Barritz, Esquires

Wm. Rombough, John Eecleston, Lemuel Standin & Frederick Creecy, Gentlemen, Freeholders & Owners of Slaves.

The Court after hearing the Evidence do say that aforementioned Negro Jacob is Guilty of Stealing the hog, do adjudge the said fellow Jacob be Carried to the Whipping Post and there receive thirty nine Lashes on his bare back and have both his Ears Nailed to the post and then Cut off.
Tho Benbury, Michl. Payne, Wm Barritz, Wm Rombough, John Eecleston, Lem Standin & Fredr. Creecy.

****

State Vs. James, a Slave
Breaking & Entering
Chowan County [1790]

Chowan County
  Complaint hath this day been made to me on Oath by William Shaw, that some time in the Month of February last he had his Store broke open and had stole from thence, one piece printed Linnen, one Bed Tyke, fourteen yards Stript holland, five pair Mens shoes, three pewter tea potts, one pound Coarse white thread and about on barrel of Northward Rum, and that he has great and probable reason to believe the said Articles were stolen from him by Jack, belonging to the Estate of John Baptist Beasley, and a Free Negroe Woman named Betty, and a Negroe Fellow named James the property the property of Mrs. Penelope Cooley
  These are therefore in the Name of the State to cause you to make diligent Search in the Kitchen & out houses of the said Beasley and Cooley in the day time, and when found to bring the same and the persons in where possession they are found in before me or some other Justice of the

Chowan County
Magistrates Courts Records

Peace to be dealt with as the Law directs, Given under my hand & Seal this 17th day of August 1790.
To any Lawfull Officer to Execute & Return
Nathl. Allen   (Seal)

You are hereby directed to Commit James the Slave named herein to the Public Goal
Edenton 7th Aug 1790
And duly Committed to Goal
Nathl. Allen

To the Sheriff of Chowan County Greeting:
    You are hereby required to summon three Justices of the Peace for the aforesaid County and four Freeholders all owners of Slaves to attend, at the Court House in Edenton at 5 o'Clock this afternoon in Order to try certain Slaves Charged with committing a Robbery in the Store of William Shaw in February last, herein fail not. Given under my hand & Seal this xxiii August 1790.
Nathl Allen   (Seal)
Summoned, Nathaniel Allen, William Barritz & Edmund Blount, Esquires.

Samuel Butler, J.H. Eelbuk, Alexander & Robert Egan, Freeholders.
Mickl. Payne

****

State Vs. John, a Slave
Attempted Arson
Chowan County [1797]

Trial of Negro John
Grant belonging to
Allen Ramsey
6th Jany. 1797

At a Court Called & held at the Court House in Edenton this 6th day of January in the year 1797 for the Trial of Negroe Man John Grants the

8

Chowan County
Magistrates Courts Records

property of Allen Ramsey Charged with having attempted to set the House of John Hornsblow on Fire

Present, the worshipfull Stephen Cabarrus, William Borritz, William Littlejohn & John Bond, Esquires & Justices.

William Saterfield, William Rombough, Thomas Seaman, King Luten, Thomas Hankins, John Vail, James Hoskins, John C. Chishire, James Saterfield, William Bains, Samuel Butler, Hamilton Warring, Owners of Slaves

The Prisoner Negro John being Charged Pleads not Guilty. The above Jury being impannelled & Sworn on this Trial Say the Prisoner is Not Guilty.

At a Court Called and held at Edenton in the Court House in Edenton this 6th day January 1797 for the Trial of Negro John Grant the property of Allen Ramsey, Charged with having Stolen a piece of Elastick Cloth &c.

Present the Worshipfull Stephen Cabarrus, William Borritz, William Littlejohn, John Bond & Samuel Dickinson, Esquires & Justices.

William Saterfield, William Rombough, Thomas Seaman, King Luton, Thomas Hankins[Hawkins], John Vail, James Hoskins, John Chishire, James Saterfield, William Bains, Samuel Butler & Hamilton Warring, Owners of Slaves

The Prisoner John Grant being Charged Pleads Not Guilty. The above Jury being impannelled & Sworn on this Trial say the Prisoner is Guilty of the Charge Contained in the Indictment whereupon the Cause passed Judgment that the Prisoner John Grant do receive Thirty Nine Lashes on his Bare Back, and that Allen Ramsey the Owner of Sd. Negro pay all Costs.

****

State Vs. Bett, a Slave
Arson
Chowan County [1797]

Chowan County
Magistrates Courts Records

Trial of Negroe Bett
Belonging to Samuel Dickinson
30th Jany 1797

At a Court Called and held at the Court House in Edenton on the 30th day of January in the year 1797 for the Trial of Negro Girl Bett the property of said Samuel Dickinson Esquire, being Charged with setting fire to the Dwelling House of said Samuel Dickinson.

Present the Worshipfull William Borritz John Mars, Jacob Blount & William Littlejohn, Esquires & Justices

Alexander Miller, Charles Laughree, Samuel Butler, Lemuel Standin, Thomas Hankins, John Little, King Luten, James [?], Thomas Satterfield, James Granberry, John Hornblow, & Honor Neil, Owners of Slaves.

The Prisoner Negroe Bett being Charged Pleads not Guilty. The above Jury being Impanelled & Sworn on this Trial Say the prisoner is Not Guilty.

Chowan County
Civil Actions

Chapter Two

Chowan County

Civil Actions

North Carolina State Archives
Chowan County Records
Miscellaneous Slave Records
C.R.024.928.3

John L. Simons Vs Thomas Simons
Civil Actions
Chowan County [1832]

John L. Simons
Petition for sale of Negroe
Thomas Simons
Filed Mar Term 1832
M H Atto pro Peto

Clk entering & Copy
Petition $ .70
2 Couten   .60
Decree & order   .75

Chowan County
Civil Actions

$2.05

T. V. Hathaway   .30
Dpy Shff
Atto MH   4.00
$6.35
.35
6.70
Clerk for selling   5.00
$11.70

To be executed on Thos. Simons & returned to June County Court. Executed by delivering a Copy of the within to Tho Simons this 13th June 1832.
Wm. Rascoe, Shff
By T.V. Hathaway, DS

State of North Carolina   } March Term 1832
Chowan County Court   }

     To the Worshipful Justices of said Court.
The Petition of John L. Simons of said County, Humbly sheweth, that your Petitioner & Thomas Simons of said County are tenants in Common of a Negroe Man Slave, named Henry, about thirty One Years old, which said Slave, your Petitioner are desirous shall be sold for the purpose of making a Division between him and said Thomas, each being intitled to one half; Your Petitioner therefor Prays, that said Negroe be Sold, at such time & Place & upon Such Terms as this Court may direct, and that the proceeds be paid over to your Petitioner, and that a Copy of this Petition, and Subpoena, be issued to said Thomas Simons to appear at next Term to Answer &c, and as in duty bound &c

Issued 12th June 1832
Malachi Haughton, Atto, Pro Peto.

     John L. Simons Vs. Thomas Simons

Chowan County
Civil Actions

A Negro of the name of Henry belonging to Eliz Simons was sold by the deft. For [?] 15 of March 1825 for the Sum of $29[?]. The negro was purchased by John Simons upon an agreement that the Negro was to be owned jointly between the deft. And plff, in Aug 1829 the deft. Conveyed to the pltff a Bill of Sale for the Negro but dated March 1825 -- on the 22nd of September 1830 the pltff conveyed to the deft. In pursuance of the original agreement the one half of Henry -- The pltff sues for the hire of henry -- he cannot recover for it in a matter cognizable from a Court of Equity, they being tenants in Common of the Negro -- the deft produces a receipt dated 6th of January 1828 in full of all demands for John L. Simons.

Mr. John Simons To Thomas Simons -- Dr.

1824
January To 2 months bord at 4 dollars pr month $8.00
1825
October To 3 months bord at 4 dollars ditto   12.00
To Washing Clothes 3 months 150 cents   1.50
1827
To 2 months bord at 4 dollars per month   8.00
To Washing 2 months 100 cents   1.00
And at other times about 3 months   12.00
1829
From December To August 1830 To 8 month bord at 4 dollars
Per month   32.00
1830
Washing 8 months at 50 cents per month   4.00
                                                           78.50
December 20 To 189 pounds of pork at $4.50 pr hundred   8.90
1831 February to 2 & 1/2 bushels of meal at 50 pr bushel
Potatoes   9.45
                                                           89.85

1825
To bord for negro Henry April 1st To twelve months my attendance and
negro woman   42.00
1827
August 7 months bord while at Granny Fillis   21.00
To my trouble carrying and fetching 4 times   4.00

Chowan County
Civil Actions

<u>1825 To 1831</u>
by Cash for Taxes at 80 cents per year   5.60

Gazette Press, Edenton, N.C.
State of North Carolina
   Be it remembered, That at a Court of Pleas and Quarter Sessions, held for the County of Chowan, at the Court House in Edenton, to wit: Decr. Term, 1831, John L. Simons by his Attorney Malachi Haughton Esq. Came before the Justices of our said Court, and brought his Suit in the following Words, Viz.

State of North Carolina
   To the Sheriff if Chowan County, Greeting:
We command you to take the body of Thomas Simons (if to be found in your bailiwick,) and him safely keep, so that you have him before the Justices of the Court of Pleas and Quarter Sessions to be held at the Court House in Edenton, in the County of Chowan, on the third Monday of December next, then and there to answer unto John L. Simons of a Plea of Trespass on the Case &c damages &c three hundred dollars.

   Herein fail not, and have you then and there this writ, and how you have executed the same. Witness Edmd. Hoskins Clerk of the said Court, at Edenton, this 3r^d Monday of September in the year of our Lord, 1831, and in the LVI year of American Independence.
Issued 12th Nov 1831
Executed Wm. D. Rascoe, Shff
Edmd. Hoskins, Clk

At December Term 1831 the Defendant by his Attorney Geo. W. Barney -- Esquire put in the following Pleas, Viz.
Genl. Issue Stat Li[?], Rip & issue
At March Term 1832, Continued by consent,
At June Term 1832, The Cause Came on to be tried, Jury Impannelled & Sworn, Find all the issues in favour of the Defendant, appeal prayed, and granted,
State of North Carolina
   I Edmund Hoskins Clerk of the Court of Pleas and Quarter Sessions in and for the County of Chowan, do hereby Certify the foregoing to be a True and perfect Transcript of the Suit named in the Caption from

Chowan County
Civil Actions

the Docket of said Court. Given under my hand and Seal of the Court at Edenton the first day of October 1832.
Edmd. Hoskins, Clk

Gazette Press, Edenton, N.C.

State of North Carolina
Chowan County
   Know all Men by these Presents, That we John L. Simons, Samuel T. Sawyer & Thomas J. Charlton are held and firmly bound unto Thomas Simons in the sum of Six hundred Dollars current money, to be paid to the said Thomas Simons his heirs, executors, administrators, or assigns; to the which payment well and truly to be made, we bind ourselves, our heirs, executors and administrators, jointly and severally, firmly by these presents, Sealed with our seals, and dated this 19th day of June 1832.
   The Condition of the above obligation is such, That whereas in a suit brought by John L. Simons against Thomas Simons in the County Court of Pleas and Quarter Sessions, held for the County of Chowan, on the third Monday in December in the sum of Three hundred Dollars, the Jury found all the issues in favor of the Defendant with costs of suit; and whereas the said John L. Simons hath prayed for, and obtained an appeal from the said judgment, to the next Superior Court of Law, to be held for the County of Chowan, on the second Monday after the fourth Monday of September next: Now in case the said John L. Simons doth well and truly prosecute his said appeal with effect, or in case he fail to be cast therein, shall well and truly pay all such damages, costs and charges, as shall be awarded against him by the said Superior Court, and also fulfill and perform the sentence, judgment and decree of the said Court; then the above obligation to be null and void, otherwise to remain in full force and virtue.
Signed and sealed in the presence of
Edmd. Hoskins
John L. Simons (Seal)
S.T. Sawyer   (Seal)
Tho. J. Charlton (Seal)

John L. Simons Receipt for $125.50

Chowan County
Civil Actions

On behalf of Henry
27 Octo. 1832

Received Edenton 27th October 1832 from Edmund Hoskins, Clerk of the County Court of Chowan the Sum of One hundred & Twenty five dollars & 50/100 in full for my one half the Amount Sales of Negroe Henry, Sold by him this day pursuant to an Order of said Court at September Term last made upon the Petition of John L. Simons vs Thomas Simons, said Negroe being purchased by me & I having given my Note & Security for the One half of the purchase money.
Test John L. Simons.

John Simons Vs. Thomas Simons
Subpoena for Plaintiff
William H Simons To Fall Term 1833
Of Chowan Supr. Court
Executed, James Long, Shff

State of North Carolina
To the Sheriff of Perquimans County, Greeting:
You are hereby commanded to summon William H Simons personally to be and appear before the Judge of our Superior Court of Law, to be held for the County of Chowan at the Court House in Edenton, on the second Monday after the fourth Monday of September next; then and there to testify and the truth to say in behalf of the Plaintiff in a certain matter of controversy in said Court depending, and then and there to be tried, wherein John Simons is Plaintiff and Thomas Simons is Defendant. And this you shall in no wise omit, under the penalty by law enjoined. Witness James Wills, Clerk of the said Court at Edenton, the second Monday after the fourth Monday of March, in the LVII year of our independence, Anno Dom. 1833
Ja: Wills, Clk

State of North Carolina }
Chowan County } June Term 1832

The answer of Thomas Simons to the Petition of John L. Simons, admits that he is tenant in common with John the petitioner of the negro

Chowan County
Civil Actions

mentioned in the petition, and he is willing he should be sold according to act of Assembly, the proceeds being equally divided.
G.W.B., Attorney for Deft.

John L. Simons Vs Thomas Simons
Subpoena for Deft., Immediately
Executed, Wm D Rascoe, Shff

Miscellany Press, Edenton, N.C.
State of North Carolina
To the Sheriff of Chowan County, Greeting:
    You are hereby commanded to summon William Simons personally to be and appear before the Judge of our Superior Court of Law, to be held for Chowan County, at the Court House in Edenton, Immediately next; then and there to testify and the truth to say in behalf of the Defendant in a certain matter of controversy in said Court depending and then and there to be tried; wherein John L. Simons is Plaintiff, and Thomas Simons is Defendant; and this you shall in no wise omit, under the penalty by law enjoined; and have you then and there this writ. Witness James Wills, Clerk of our said Court, the 9th day of October in the LVII year of the Independence of the United States, A.D. 1832.
Ja: Wills, Clk

Thos. Simons Receipt, $125.50

Rec'd Edenton 2 Jany 1833 from Edmund Hoskins Clerk of Chowan County Court, John L. Simons Note with Security for the sum of one hundred & twenty five dollars & fifty Cents, being one half of the Sale of Negroe Henry, Sold according to a decree of said Court at Sept. Term 1832
Thomas Simons.

John L. Simons Vs Thomas Simons
Subpoena, Wm Simons, for Plf, Immediately
Executed, Wm. D. Rascoe, Shff

Miscellany Press, Edenton, N.C.
State of North Carolina

Chowan County
Civil Actions

To the Sheriff of Chowan County, Greeting:
You are hereby commanded to summon William Simons personally to be and appear before the Judge of our Superior Court of Law, to be held for Chowan County, at the Court House in Edenton, Immediately next; then and there to testify and the truth to say in behalf of the Plaintiff in a certain matter of controversy in said Court depending and then and there to be tried, wherein John L. Simons is Plaintiff, and Thomas Simons is Defendant; and this you shall in no wise omit, under the penalty by law enjoined; and have you then and there this writ. Witness James Wills, Clerk of our said Court, the 9th day of October in the LVII year of the Independence of the United States, A.D. 1832
Ja. Wills, Clk

Simons Vs Simons
Notice, To be Returned
Executed by delivering a Copy of this Notice to John Simons
8th Octr. 1833
Wm D Rascoe, Shff

To John L. Simons, you are hereby notified to produce on the Trial of the case now pending in Chowan Superior Court the original agreement entered into Deed bearing date 22 of September 1830 whereby it is agreed that Negro man Henry should be held Jointly between us or a Copy will be offered in evidence
October 1833
Thos Simons by his Atto Jesse Wilson

John L. Simons Vs Thomas Simons
Subpoena, Wm Jones for Pltff Immediately
Executed, Wm. D. Rascoe, Shff

Miscellany Press, Edenton, N.C.
State of North Carolina
To the Sheriff of Chowan County, Greeting:
You are hereby commanded to summon William Jones personally to be and appear before the Judge of our Superior Court of Law, to be held for Chowan County, at the Court House in Edenton, Immediately next; then and there to testify and the truth to say in behalf of the Defendant in a

Chowan County
Civil Actions

certain matter of controversy in said Court depending and then and there to be tried, wherein John L. Simons is Plaintiff, and Thomas Simons is Defendant; and this you shall in no wise omit, under the penalty by law enjoined; and have you then and there this writ. Witness James Wills, Clerk of our said Court, the 12th day of October in the LVII year of the Independence, A.D. 1832
Ja: Wills, Clk

John L. Simons Vs Thomas Simons
Subpoena, James Evans for Defendant
Immediately

Miscellany Press, Edenton, N.C.
State of North Carolina
To the Sheriff of Chowan County, Greeting:
    You are hereby commanded to summon James Evans personally to be and appear before the Judge of our Superior Court of Law, to be held for Chowan County, at the Court House in Edenton Immediately next; then and there to testify and the truth to say in behalf of the Defendant in a certain matter of controversy in said Court depending and then and there to be tried, wherein John Simons is Plaintiff, and Thomas Simons is Defendant; and this you shall in no wise omit, under the penalty by law enjoined; and have you then and there this writ. Witness James Wills, Clerk of our said Court, the 12th day of October in the **[Blank]** year of the Independence of the United States, A.D. 1832.
Ja: Wills, Clk

John L. Simons Vs Thomas Simons
Subpoena Jno Gregory
Immediately

State of North Carolina
To the Sheriff of Chowan County Greeting:
    You are hereby commanded to summon John Gregory personally to be and appear before the Judge of our Superior Court of Law, to be held for the County of Chowan at the Court House in Edenton Immediately; then and there to testify and the truth to say in behalf of the Plaintiff in a certain matter of controversy in said Court depending, and then and there

Chowan County
Civil Actions

to be tried, wherein John L. Simons is Plaintiff and Thomas Simons is Defendant. And this you shall in no wise omit, under the penalty by law enjoined. Witness James Wills Clerk of the said Court at Edenton, the second Monday after the fourth Monday of March in the LVIII year of our Independence, Anno Dom. 1833.
Ja Wills, Clk

John L. Simons Vs Thomas Simons
Subpoena, Baker Hoskins for Plf, Immediately
Executed, Wm. D. Rascoe, Shff

Miscellany Press, Edenton, N.C.
State of North Carolina
To the Sheriff of Chowan County, Greeting:
    You are hereby commanded to summon Baker Hoskins personally to be and appear before the Judge of our Superior Court of Law, to be held for Chowan County, at the Court House in Edenton, Immediately next; then and there to testify and the truth to say in behalf of the Plaintiff in a certain matter of controversy in said Court depending and then and there to be tried, wherein John L. Simons is Plaintiff, and Thomas Simons is Defendant; and this you shall in no wise omit, under the penalty by law enjoined; and have you then and there this writ. Witness James Wills, Clerk of our said Court, the 8th day of October in the LVII year of the Independence of the United States, A.D. 1832
Ja: Wills, Clk

Executed for W.D. Rascoe, Shff
By B Hathaway, DS

State of North Carolina
To the Sheriff of Chowan County Greeting:
    You are hereby commanded to summon Edwin Bond personally to be and appear before the Judge of our Superior Court of Law, at the Court House in Edenton Immediately next, then and there to testify and the truth to say in behalf of the Defendant in a certain matter of controversy before said Court depending, and then and there to be tried, wherein John Simons is Plaintiff and Thomas Simons is Defendant. And this you shall in no wise omit, under the penalty by law enjoined. Witness James Wills,

Chowan County
Civil Actions

Clerk of our said Court at Edenton, the second Monday after the fourth Monday of September in the LVIII year of our Independence, A.D. 1833.
Ja Wills, Clk

John L. Simons Vs Thomas Simons
Wm Rea for Deft., Immediately
Wm. D. Rascoe, Shff

Miscellany Press, Edenton, N.C.
State of North Carolina
To the Sheriff of Chowan County, Greeting:
  You are hereby commanded to summon William Rea personally to be and appear before the Judge of our Superior Court of Law, to be held for Chowan County, at the Court House in Edenton Immediately next; then and there to testify and the truth to say in behalf of the Defendant in a certain matter of controversy in said Court depending and then and there to be tried, wherein John L. Simons is Plaintiff, and Thomas Simons is Defendant; and this you shall in no wise omit, under the penalty by law enjoined; and have you then and there this Writ. Witness James Wills, Clerk of our said Court, the 12th day of October in the LVII year of the Independence of the United States, A.D. 1832
Ja: Wills, Clk

John L. Simons Vs Thomas Simons
Appeal & Transcript, Fall Term 1832

Witness for Pltff
Jno M. Woodward, Perquimans & Wm Simons, B. Hoskins & T. Skinner
For Defendant, Wm Jones, Wm Rea & James Evans

Judgment for Defendant	
Clk	$4.15
Appeal	2.80
	$6.95
Shff Chowan	3.25
Do Perq	0.30
Witness Wm Jones	1.46
Do Wm Rea	1.30

Chowan County
Civil Actions

Atto GWB	4.00
	$17.26

Appeal	
Fi Fa	
10 Sub	
Seal	3.65
Sheriff	2.10
Shff of Perquimans	30
Witness Baker Hoskins	6.03
Wm Rea	5.60
Wm Jones	86
Jno Gregory	7.93
Wm Simons	11.88

Chowan County
Criminal Actions

Chapter Three

Chowan County

Criminal Actions

North Carolina State Archives
Chowan County Records
Miscellaneous Slave Records
C.R.024.928.3

State Vs Certain Slaves
Criminal Actions
Outlawry
Chowan County [1816]

Writ of Outlawry Vs Negro Slaves Jacob, Dilworth, Peter, Jack, Henry, Abram & Thompson

State of North Carolina } Court of Pleas and Quarter Sessions
Chowan County   } December Term 1816

      By Nathaniel C. Bissell, Thomas Jones, John McGuire, Reuben Small, Henry Flury, James Sutton, Nathaniel Bond, Edmund Hoskins, Exum Simpson and William Baines Esquires.

Chowan County
Criminal Actions

Whereas complaint hath this day been made to us Justices of the Peace for the said County that the following negro Slaves, to wit, Jacob the property of the Honourable Henry Seawell Esquire, Dilworth the property of John Bond, Peter and Jack the property of William Simons, Jim the property of William Rascoe, Henry the property of Micajah Bunch, Esquire, Sam the property of Josiah Skinner, Abram the property of Captain John Lanston and Thompson the property of Edward C Outlaw & Sampson the property of Henderson Standin's Administrator have absented themselves from the Service of their respective Masters, and are lurking about in the County committing many acts of felony. These are therefore in the name of the State to command the aforesaid Slaves to surrender themselves to their respective Masters. And we do hereby command the Sheriff of the said County of Chowan to make diligent search and pursuit after the above mentioned Slaves and them and either of them having found to apprehend and secure, so that they may be conveyed to their respective Masters, or otherwise discharged as the law directs. And the said Sheriff is hereby empowered to raise and take with him such power of his County as he shall think fit for apprehending the said Slaves. And we do hereby by virtue of an act of Assembly in this State concerning Servants and Slaves, intimate and declare & the aforenamed negro Slaves do not surrender themselves and return home immediately after the publication of these presents, that any person or persons may kill and destroy the said Slaves and either of them, by such means as he or they may think proper without accusation or impeachment of any crime or offence for so doing or without incurring any penalty or forfeiture thereby. [Torn]erty of John Coffield

Given under our hands and seals at the Court House in Edenton the 12th day of december in the year of our Lord one thousand eight hundred and sixteen.

Nathl Bissell, JP (Seal), Thos Jones, JP, (Seal), Jno McGuire, JP,(Seal), Reuben Small, JP, (Seal), Henry Flury, JP, (Seal), James Sutton, JP, (Seal), Nathl Bond, JP, (Seal), Edmd Hoskins, JP, (Seal), Exum Simpson, JP, (Seal), William Baines, JP, (Seal).

****

State Vs Anthony Adams
Criminal Actions

Chowan County
Criminal Actions

Misdemeanor
Chowan County [1856]

State Vs Anthony Adams
Misdemeanor
A True Bill
Martin B Simpson, Foreman
Chas Robinson, Sworn & Sent
Wm. R. Skinner, Clk

The Grand Jurors upon their oath present Anthony Adams that calls himself a free man, for migrating into this State.
Martin B Simpson, Foreman

State of North Carolina } Court of Pleas & Quarter Sessions
Chowan County   } August Term 1856

  The Jurors for the State on their oath present that Anthony Adams a free man of colour not being a citizen of this State did on the 1st day of July 1856 migrate into this State contrary to the form of the Statute in such case made & provided.
  The Jurors aforesaid on their oath aforesaid do further present that Anthony Adams a free man of colour not being a citizen of this State & coming into this State as a Sailor did on the 1st day of June 1856 attempt & did migrate into this State by quitting the vessel in which he came into the State & not leaving the State in the same contrary to the form of the Statute in such case made & provided.
E.C. Hines, Solicitor

State Vs. Anthony Adams
Capias, Nov Term 1856
Executed, P.F. White, Shff

State of North Carolina
To the Sheriff of Chowan County, Greeting:
  You are hereby commanded to take the body of Anthony Adams (if to be found un your County) and safely keep, so that you have him

Chowan County
Criminal Actions

before the Justices of our Court of Pleas and Quarter Sessions, to be held for the County of Chowan at the Court House in Edenton on the 1st Monday in November next, then and there to answer unto the State of N. Carolina by our solicitor E.C. Hines Esq. Concerning an offense which he committed & whereof he stands charged by bill of indictment found by our Grand Jurors at August Term last. Herein fail not, and have you then and there this writ. Witness, William R. Skinner, Clerk of our said Court, at Office in Edenton on the 1st Monday in August and in the 81st year of our Independence, Anno Dom. 1856.
Issued the 24th day of September 1856
Wm R. Skinner, Clerk

State Vs. Adams
Subpoena, Nov Term 1856
For Pltff, C.E. Robinson
Executed, PF White, Shff

State of North Carolina
To the Sheriff of Chowan County, Greeting:
    You are hereby commanded to summon Charles E. Robinson personally to be and appear before the Court of P. & Q. Sessions, at the Court House in Edenton, 1st Monday in November, then and there to testify and the truth to say in a certain matter of controversy before said Court depending Vs Anthony Adams. And this you shall in no wise omit, under the penalty by law enjoined.
    Witness, William R. Skinner, Clerk of the Court of Pleas and Quarter Sessions, at Edenton, the First Monday in August 1856, and in the 81st year of our Independence.
Issued the 24th Day of September 1856
Wm R. Skinner, Clerk.

****

State Vs. Richard Wynns
Criminal Actions
Misdemeanor
Chowan County [1856]

A True Bill

Chowan County
Criminal Actions

Martin B Simpson, Foreman
Witnesses, Chas E Robinson
Sworn & Sent
Wm R. Skinner, Clk

State Vs. Richard Wynns
Capias, Nov Term 1856
Not to be found in my County
P.F. White, Shff

State of North Carolina
To the Sheriff of Chowan County, Greeting:
You are hereby commanded to take the body of Richard Wynns (if to be found in your County) and him safely keep, so that you have him before the Justices of our Court of Pleas and Quarter Sessions, to be held for the County of Chowan at the Court House in Edenton on the 1st Monday in November next, then and there to answer unto the State of N. Carolina concerning an offence which he Committed & whereof he stands charged by bill of Indictment found by our Grand Jurors at August Term last. Herein fail not, and have you then and there this writ. Witness, William R. Skinner, Clerk of our said Court, at Office in Edenton on the 1st Monday in August and in the 81st year of our Independence, Anno Dom. 1856.
Issued the 26th Day of September 1856.
Wm R Skinner, Clerk.

State Vs Richard Wynns
Capias, Febry Term 1857
Not to be found in my County
PF White, Shff

State of North Carolina
To the Sheriff of Chowan County, Greeting:
You are hereby commanded to take the body of Richard Wynns (if to be found in your County) and him safely keep, so that you have him before the Justices of our Court of Pleas and Quarter Sessions, to be held for the County of Chowan at the Court House in Edenton on the 1st Monday in February next, then and there to answer unto the State of N. Carolina concerning an offence which he committed & whereof he stands

Chowan County
Criminal Actions

charged. Herein fail not, and have you then and there this writ. Witness, William R. Skinner, Clerk of our said Court, at Office in Edenton on the 1st Monday in Nov and in the 81st year of our Independence, Anno Dom. 1856.
Issued the 21st Day of Jany 1857
Wm. R. Skinner, Clerk

State Vs. Richard Wynns
Capias, June Term 1857
Not to be found
P F White, Shff

State of North Carolina
To the Sheriff of Chowan County -- Greeting:
    You are hereby commanded to take the body of Richard Wynns (if to be found in your County) and him safely keep, so that you have him before the Justices of our Court of Pleas and Quarter Sessions to be held for the County of Chowan, at the Court House in Edenton, on the 3rd Monday in June next, then and there to answer unto the State of N. Carolina concerning an offence of migrating into this State, whereof he stands charged by bill of Indictment. Herein fail not, and have you then and there this writ. Witness, William R. Skinner, Clerk of our said Court, at Office in Edenton, on the 4th Monday in March and in the 81st year of our Independence, Anno Domini 1857.
Issued the 9th Day of June 1857
Wm. R. Skinner, Clerk

State Vs. Richard Wynns
Capias, March Term 1857
Not to be found
P.F. White, Shff

State of North Carolina
To the Sheriff of Chowan County -- Greeting:
    You are hereby commanded to take the body of Richard Wynns (if to be found in your County) and him safely keep, so that you have him before the Justices of our Court of Pleas and Quarter Sessions to be held for the County of Chowan, at the Court House in Edenton, on the 4th

Chowan County
Criminal Actions

Monday in March next, then and there to answer unto the State of North Carolina concerning an offence of migrating into this State, whereof he stands Charged by bill of Indictment. Herein fail not, and have you then and there this Writ. Witness, William R. Skinner, Clerk of our said Court, at Office in Edenton, on the first Monday in February, Anno Domini 1857. Issued the 4th Day of March 1857.
Wm. R. Skinner, Clerk.

State Vs. Richard Wynns
Subpoena, Nov Term 1856 for Pltff
Chas. Robinson
Executed P.F. White, Shff

State of North Carolina
To the Sheriff of Chowan County, Greeting:
    You are hereby commanded to summon Charles Robinson personally to be and appear before the Court of P. & Q. Sessions, at the Court House in Edenton on the 1st Monday in Nov next, then and there to testify and the truth to say in a certain matter before said Court depending Vs Richard Wynns. And this you shall in no wise omit, under the penalty by law enjoined.
    Witness, William R. Skinner, Clerk of the Court of Pleas and Quarter Sessions, at Edenton, the First Monday in August 1856, and in the 81st year of our Independence.
Issued 24th Day of September 1856.
Wm R Skinner, Clerk.

State Vs. Richard Wynn
Subpoena, March Term 1857 for Pltff
Chas E. Robinson

State of North Carolina
To the Sheriff of Chowan County, Greeting:
    We command you to summon Charles E. Robinson personally be and appear before our next Court of Pleas and Quarter Sessions, to be held for the County of Chowan, at the Courthouse in Edenton, on the 4th Monday of March next, then and there to testify and the truth to say in behalf of the Plaintiff in a certain matter of controversy in our said Court

Chowan County
Criminal Actions

depending between the State of N. Carolina, Plaintiff, and Richard Wynns (of Color) Defendant. Herein fail not under the penalty prescribed by law.
Witness -- William R. Skinner, Clerk of our said Court at Office in Edenton, the first Monday of February A.D. 1857.
Issued the 4th Day of March A.D. 1857
Wm R Skinner, Clerk.

****

State Vs. Peter Cain
Criminal Actions
Misdemeanor
Chowan County [1859]

State Vs Peter Cain
In'd migrating into State
Genl Pros, Chas Robinson
Sworn & sent
W.R. Skinner, Clk
A True Bill, Jos T Waff, Fore.

State of N. Carolina   } Court of Pleas & Quarter Sessions
Chowan County   } Augt. Term 1859

     The Jurors for the State upon their oath present that on the first day of January 1859 a free negro named Peter Cain did migrate down from the State of Virginia into the County of Chowan in the State of North Carolina and from that time has continuously resided in the said County of Chowan, State aforesaid Contrary to the form of the Statute in such case provided & against the peace & dignity of the State
Mr S. Hawks, Sol.

State Vs Peter Cain
Executed by P F White, Shff
By C. E. Robinson, Dep. Shff

State of North Carolina   }
Chowan County   }

Chowan County
Criminal Actions

To the Sheriff of Chowan County you are hereby commanded to arrest the body of Peter Cain & have him before me or some other Justice of the Peace of this County for migrating into this State agt. the Statute made & provided in such cases.
Given under my hand & seal this 24th June 1859.
[?] JP   (Seal)

*Chowan County
Gun Permits*

Chapter Four

Chowan County

Gun Permits

**North Carolina State Archives
Chowan County Records
Miscellaneous Slave Records
C.R.024.928.3**

H. Standin to the Court
Bond for negroe Harry to Carry a Gun
To be Renewed

State of North Carolina }
Chowan County   }

    Know all Men by these Presents that we Henderson Standin & James Sutton are held and firmly Bound unto Stephen Cabarrus Esqr. Chairman of the County Court of Chowan in the Sum of two hundred & fifty Pounds to which payment well & Truly to be made and done we bind our Selves, Our heirs, Executors & Administrators Jointly & Severally firmly by these Presents, Sealed with our Seals & Dated this 16th day of Decr. 1797.

Chowan County
Gun Permits

The Condition of the above obligation is such that if a Certain Negroe Called Harry the Property of the said Henderson Standin who is allowed to Carry Court of Chowan shall well & Truly Demean himself and do no Injury with his said Gun to any Person or Persons whatever then this obligation to be Void or else to remain in full force & Virtue.
Hendr. Standin   (Seal)
James Sutton   (Seal)
Signed Sealed & Delivered in Presence of
B.N. [?]

****

Benjamin Brown
Bond for Negroe Merick to Carry a Gun
March 98

State of North Carolina   }

Know all men by these Presents that we Benjamin Brown & Henderson Standin are held & firmly bound unto Charles Johnson Esqr. Chairman & the Rest of the Justices of Chowan County Court in the just & full Sum of two hundred & fifty Pounds to the which payment well & Truly to be made & done we Bind our Selves & Each of our heirs, Executors & Administrators Jointly & Severally, firmly by these Presents, Sealed with our Seals & dated this 15th Day of March 1798.

The Condition of the above obligation is such that whereas the above Bounden Benjamin Brown hath obtained leave of this Worshipfull Court for his Negro man Merick to Carry a Gun on his said Masters Land - he shall well & Truly demean himself and do no Injury with his said Gun to any Person or Persons whatever then this obligation to be Void Else to Remain in full force & virtue
B. Brown   (Seal)
Hendr. Standin   (Seal)
Signed, Seald & Delivrd in presence of [?]fleet

****

James Hathaway Esqr.
To Court

Chowan County
Gun Permits

Bond for Negroe Derry to Carry a Gun
March 1804

The Subscriber finds himself under many disadvantages attending him from not having any Person Priviledged to Keep a gun on his quarter, he therefore Prays the Worshipfull Court of the County of Chowan to grant him Liberty for his negro Slave by Name Derry to Carry a gun on his own Plantation
Jas. Hathaway
March 18th day 1804

Fully substantiated, Agreement date of - Swa[?] Testimony - large heap of Manure - Articles & Boors labour - not in Mr Cummings [?] power - take same into his Hands estimating Damages - no man can direct another of property without Answering - resort to [?] or caprice[?] - justify by non Paymt of Rent - demand of Security - why not pay - [?] out of possession - 1st Day of Jany demanded but not due

State of No. Carolina }
Chowan County   }

    Know all men by these presents that we James Hathaway and Thomas Browning are held and firmy bound unto Stephen Cabarrus Esqr. Chairman of the County Court of Chowan in the sum of two hundred and fifty pounds to which payment well and truly to be made and done we bind ourselves our heirs, Exrs. And Administrators Jointly and severally firmly by these presents sealed with our seals & dated this 14th day of March 1804.

    The Condition of the above obligation is such that if a certain negro called Derry the property of the said James Hathaway who is allowed to carry a Gun on his said Masters Land by the County Court of Chowan shall well and truly demean himself and do no injury with his said Gun to any person or persons whatever then the obligation to be void or else to remain in full force and virtue
Jas. Hathaway, Senr.   (Seal)
Thos Browning   (Seal)
Signed sealed and delivered in presence of
G.T. Goodman

Chowan County
Gun Permits

****

H: Standen
To the Court
Bond for Negro Harry to carry a Gun

State of North Carolina }
Chowan County   }

    Know all men by these presents that we Henderson Standen & James Sutton are held & firmly bound unto Stephen Cabarrus Esqr. Chairman of the County Court of Chowan in the sum of two Hundred & fifty pounds to the which payment well & truly to be made and done we Bind our Selves our heirs, Executors & Administrators Jointly & Severally firmly by these presents Sealed with our Seals and dated the 12th day of September 1806.

    The Condition of the above Obligation is such that if a Certain Negroe Man Called Harry the property of Henderson Standen, who is allowed to Carry a Gun on his Masters Land, by the County Court of Chowan shall well & Truly demean himself and do no injury with his said Gun to any person or Persons whatever then this obligation to be Void or Else to remain in full force & virtue.

Hendr. Standen   (Seal)
James Sutton   (Seal)
Signed Sealed & Delivered in presence of
[?]

****

Saml. Tredwell
To the Court
Bond for Negro to carry a Gun
June Term 1807

State of North Carolina }
Chowan County   }

    Know all men by these presents that we Samuel Tredwell & Duncan McDonald are held and firmly bound unto Stephen Cabarrus Esqr.

Chowan County
Gun Permits

Chairman of the County Court of Chowan in the sum of Two hundred & fifty pounds to the which payment well and truly to be made and done we bind ourselves our heirs executors & administrators jointly & severally firmly by these presents Sealed with our Seals and dated the 13th day of June 1807.

The Condition of the above obligation is such that if a certain negro man called Harry the property of Samuel Tredwell, who is allowed to carry a gun on his masters land, by the County Court of Chowan shall well & Truly demean himself and do no injury with his said gun to any person or persons whatever then this obligation to be void or else to remain in full force and virtue
Saml. Tredwell (Seal)
Dn. McDonald (seal)
Signed, Sealed & delivered in presence of
[?]

****

Elisha Copeland
To the Court
Petition

To the right honourable Justices of the December term of Chowan County Court.
  The humble Petition of Elisha Copeland of Edenton, County of Chowan Sheweth
  That your Petitioner is in [?] of permission to place in the hands of his negro man Limbrick a Gun a quarter of a pound of Powder & a pound of Shot for the use of his farm whereon said negro resides.
  Your Petitioner therefore humbly Prays that he may be permitted so to do and your Petitioner shall ever Pray.
Elisha Copeland

****

Wm Wright
Petr to Court
For Negro man Davy to Carry a Gun
March Term 1830, allowed

Chowan County
Gun Permits

To the Worshipfull County Court of Pleas and Quarter Sessions for the County of Chowan.

Your Petitioner Prays your Worshipfull Body to grant him an Order, for his Negro Slave named Davy (who is the foreman on his farm in Green Hall under the direction of Mr. John Blount) that the said Negroe Slave may Carry a Gun on his said Farm to protect his Crop from the Crows, Birds &c. and that I Bind my Self to make good any damage that may be done by the said Gun, and your Petitioner will ever Pray &c.
Wm. Wright
Edenton March 15th 1830
Prayer of the Petitioner granted.

*Chowan County
Patrol Records*

Chapter Five

Chowan County

Patrol Records

**North Carolina State Archives
Chowan County Records
Miscellaneous Slave Records
C.R.024.928.3**

June Term 1784

Order for Jonathan Boulton, Robert Hohns, Mason Miller & Henderson Luten, Patrolers

State of North Carolina } Chowan County Court
Chowan County   } Anno Domini 1784

     Present the Worshipful Justices
Ordered that Jonathan Boulton, Robert Hohns[**Holms**], Henderson Luten senr. And Mason Miller be Appointed Patrolers in Captain Bonds District They truly Observing the Acts of Assembly in Such Cases made and provided
Test Will Wilkins for James Blount CCC

Chowan County
Patrol Records

****

Petition of Lemuel Creecy & others
Septr 1785

September 26th 1785
To the Worshipfull Court now Sitting
May it please your Worships, We the Subscribers think Necessary as Well for the benefit of our Neighbours As our Selves, that their Shoud be Patrolers appointed For keeping the Negroes in better Subjection although there is Patrolers appointed, Very few of them do their duty, by Which Means there is a number Of Negroes Passing & repassing at all times of the Night Without Liberty from their Owners much to the injury of our property, therefore We the Subscribers Humbly pray you'd Appointed us Patrolers, requesting no indulgence or Exemptions for our Service
Leml. Creecy, Fred Creecy, Richard Benbury & Nathan Creecy.

****

State of North Carolina } Chowan County Court
} March Term 98

This may Certify that Edmond Norcom was appointed a Patroler at March term 1797
Test. [?]fleet

Ticket for Attending as Patroler, $4, 1799

Edenton January 23rd 1797, A List of 24 Companies of Patrolers.

No. 6 Nathl Allen Capt, Wm Carter, Honore Neil & John Humphris,
No 12 Jacob Blount, Capt, John Chishers, Francis Beasley & Alexr Millin
No 22 Josiah Collins, Senr. Capt, Hamelton Warren, Henry King & Miles Badham
No 10 Michal Payne, Capt, Thos. Iredell, Joseph Deakings & George Campbell
No 20 William Littlejohn, Capt., John Blount, Jonathan Malbee & James Wills

Chowan County
Patrol Records

No 19 James Hathaway, Capt, G: N. Phillips, Hezekiah Gorham, Timothy Tomson
No 24 James Granbery, Capt., Thomas B. Littlejohn, Thomas Johnson
No 1 Samuel Butler, Capt., Henderson Luten, C.W. Janson & Edward Reily
No 13 John Little, Capt., Allen Ramsey, Wm Black & Thomas Sanderlin
No 5 George Morgan, Capt., James Boyce, Benjn.Norfleet, Burton Hathaway
No 4 John Mare, Capt., James Ward, Henry Warrick, & John Spooner
No 14 Samuel Dickinson, Capt., Henry Kennedy, John Borritz & Samuel Smith
No 18 Fredrick Rameekee, Capt., Clement Hall, Francis Jones & Saml. Wilkins
No 7 Jeremiah Gallop, Capt., William Lowree, John Nail & Roger Squires
No 23 Thomas Hankins, Capt., Josiah Collins Junr., John Badham & Ebenezer Paine
No 17 E Norfleet, Capt., Nathan Bixley, Wm. Edwards & John Popelston
No 15 Myles O.Malley, Capt., John Bennett, Geo: Wilkinson & John Fife
No 2 William Rombough, Capt., Edmund Hoskins, James Neill & James Saterfield.
No 3 Thomas Seaman, Capt., Clement Hall, Francis Jones & Saml. Wilkins
No 11 Henry Wills, Capt., Henry Gardner, John Williams & Charles Laughree
No 9 Thomas Waff, Capt., Wm. Saterfield, Thomas Saterfield & David Humphries
No 16 Robert Moody, Capt., Joseph Bozman, Henderson Standin, & Martin Skeels
No 21 Thomas Bissell, Capt., Ivy Purdie, William Wyate & Thomas Whidbee
No 8 King Luten, Capt., John Beasley, Fredrick Blount & Solomon Ward

****

State Vs. the Patrolers, Citation, December Term 97

State of North Carolina Chowan County
To the Sheriff of Chowan County Greeting

Chowan County
Patrol Records

You are hereby required to Summon the following Persons Patrolers, to be and appear before the worshipfull the County Court to be held on the second Monday in December Instant 1797.

William Gregory, Edward Haughton, Eli Bertie, Robt Donalson, Thomas W. Thomson, Joseph Bunch, Moses Buckley, James Jackson, Isaac Welch, Richard Skinner, Thomas Waff, Thomas Saterfield, Wm Saterfield, Abraham Hassel, John Pettyjohn, Edm Norcom, Richard Ming, Thomas Jones, Samuel M Guire, Myles Eliot, Cullen Halsey, Henry Kennedy, Zachariah Webb & Francis Beasley

Decr 4th 1797 By directions of the States atto
E Norfleet, CCC

****

Patrolers in Capt Skinners District
September 98

State of North Carolina   } Chowan County Court
                           } September Term 1798

Ordered that John Hoskins, Josiah Jones, William Deal, William Goodwin, John M Guyer, William Newborn be appointed Patrolers in Capt. Skinners District for Twelve Months, thay Strictly attending to the act of assembly a Copy of which is here with sent them - By order
Test, E Norfleet, CCC

To James Jackson Constable
You are hereby required, to inform the above named Persons, of their being appointed Patrolers, & to read the inclosed Copy of the act of assembly to Each one & deliver it to some one of the six appointed.
By order of the Court
Test. E Norfleet, CCC

****

List of Patrolers in Capt. Cullens District
September 98

Chowan County
Patrol Records

State of North Carolina } Chowan County Court
} September Term 1798

Ordered that Moses Hobbs, John Perry, John Felton, Jacob Cullens, Harmon Hurdle, Henry Hurdle be appointed Patrolers in Capt Cullins District for twelve months - they Strictly attending to the Act of Assembly a Copy of which they have herewith
By Order Test. E Norfleet, CCC

To Moses Hobbs, Constable you are hereby required to inform the rest of the above named Persons, of their being appointed Patrolers, & to Read the indorsed Copy of the act of Assembly, to Each one, and then deliver it to some one of the six or Keep it as you may agree among your Selves.
By Order of the Court
Test. E Norfleet, CCC

****

State of North Carolina } Chowan County Court
} June Term 1804

This Certifys that Archibald Leath was appointed as one of the Patrole for the ensuing Yeare in the Town of Edenton
Test George Waff

Rec'd of Charles Roberts forty shillings in full for the Within Orders
Archibald Leath
A. Leath, Receipt 40/ for Patrol

****

Warrant for Patrolers in Capt. Smalls District

State of North Carolina } Chowan County Court
} June Term 1800

Ordered that the following persons be Appointed as Patrolers in Capt Smalls District for one year Viz

Chowan County
Patrol Records

Benjamin Coffield, James Jones, Francis Briols, Thomas Mathias, David Small & Nathanl. Howcott

They Strictly Adhearing to the Act of Assembly
Test. E Norfleet, CCC

****

Order of Court for the Patrolers

State of North Carolina } Chowan County Court
 } September Term 1800

Ordered that William Ming, John Perry, Jacob Jordan, Moses Hobbs, William Bush, & Jacob Cullins be appointed Patrolers in Capt. Cullins District for one year
Test. E Norfleet, CC

****

Ordered that the Persons within named be appointed Patrolers

John Bush, Benja. Bateman, Paul Bunch, James Evans & John Boyce be appointed patrols on the west side of the Va road in Capt Pains District

****

Miles Wright of Chowan Co. Wish in the [?] a Company of Patrol, appointed consisting of Miles Wright, Willis Welch, [?], Wm. Bush, Timothy [?], George F Hutton

****

Patroll Certificate, 1804

State of North Carolina }
Chowan County }

This Certifys John Fife Served as Capt. Of the Patrole in the year 1804 in my stead

Chowan County
Patrol Records

George Waff

****

Petition, Septr Term 1827
September Term 1827

To the Worshipfull Corte Now sitting Will Grant an Order that Eah[?] Elliot Esq Co to Myles Wright, William Jackson and John Boush be appointed to [?] and Settle the Estate of John Parish Dec'd and make report to the next term.
William Walton

****

Certificate for Allen Lasiter &c 1806 $6.0

State of North Carolina }
Chowan County }

This is to Certify that Allen Lasiter was Appointed Capt. Of the Patrole for the year 1806, and that, Miles Hassell, Samuel Rea & Moses Webb is returned by him as his Company
Test. E Norfleet, CCC

****

State of North Carolina }
Chowan County Court } September Term 1810

Ordered that Richard Bond be appointed Captain of the Patrole in Capt Bonds District in the room and stead of Edward Haughton resigned and that he appoint five other persons to Act with him
Test Jas. Norfleet, Clk

****

This may Certify that John Bond Junr. Has Patroled on year, from June 1803 to June 1804.
Richd. Hoskins, C.P.

Chowan County
Patrol Records

****

State of North Carolina }
Chowan County Court } Novr. Term 1846

Ordered that the Clerk furnish to each Chairman of the patrol District & to each Captain of the patrol a Copy of the following Regulations to wit: Rules for the Government of the patrols.

1st The Captains of each patrol Company shall ride out their Companies at least three nights in Two Weeks and as much oftener as the Captains may deem proper.

2nd In the absences of the Captains, by Sickness or other unavoidable Cause. The Company may appoint any other member of their body to act as Captain protemp

3rd If the Captain shall neglect two weeks in succession to call out the patrol, he shall forfeit for each neglect the Sum of Five Dollars and all Claims and Compensation for his Services, unless he shall have some Satisfactory excuse for such neglect to be approved of by the Court, and it is hereby made the duty of the other members of the Patrol to report to the Court the neglect of the Captain to discharge the duties hereby enjoined upon him under the penalty of forfeiting their Claims to Compensation, in the event of their neglecting to do so.

4th Any member of the patrol [Faded] has the power of hireing a substitute whenever he or they may be prevented attending by Sickness or otherwise.

5th Every member of the patrol failing to attend at the time and place appointed by the Captain shall forfeit for each neglect the sum of Two Dollars unless his or their absence shall be excused by the Captain.

6th It shall be the duty of each Captain of every patrol to report to the Court at the expiration of the year for which the patrol is appointed the number of times that each one his Company shall have failed to discharge his or their duty and the amount or amounts forfeited for such neglect shall be deducted out of the Compensation hereby allowed the patrol and

Chowan County
Patrol Records

deduction shall be made out of the Compensation allowed the Captains of all forfeitures that he may have incurred by any neglect of duty on his part.

7th Each member of the patrol who shall faithfully discharge the duties imposed by the act of Assembly in that case made and provided, & the duties hereby required of them shall at the extermination of the year from the time of his or their appointment be entitled to receive the Sum of Twenty Dollars.

8th Any one of the patrols shall when it is necessary act alone.

A True Copy
Teste. T. V. Hathaway, Clk

To be left with the Captain of the Patrol in the Middle District
We the Committee are satisfied that the Patrol in the Middle District consisting of Calep Perry, Capt., Miles Goodwin, T. Cochran, Alfred Boyce, Richd. Goodwin & Jos T Waff have discharged their duty as a Patrol for the Present year Saml Simps, Martin B. [?], William J Halley

Notify the Committee that these arrangements are done, allowed Twenty Dollars each

****

[Patrollers, District not given]

Saml Butler, John Blount, Joseph Bozman, Josiah Collins, Thomas Cox, Henry Flury[?], Joseph Fereboult, James Hathaway, John Horniblow, Thomas Hankins, John Little, Nathaniel Allen, Charles Laughre, King Luten, Thos B. Littlejohn, Myles O Mally, George Morgan, Alexander Miller[**Millen** ?], Honore Neill, James Niel, John Popleston, Edwd. Reily, William Rombough, Henderson Standin, Wm Saterfield, Thomas Seaman, Thomas Saterfield, Roger Squire, Zachariah Webb, Henry Wills, George Wilkinson, Hambleton Warring, Henry Eelbeck.

****

Capt. Norcoms District

Chowan County
Patrol Records

Lemuel Burket, Joseph C. Benbury, George Beasley - Patroler, Robert Bertie, William Bains, Robert Beasley, Geo: Baines Senr, John Blount, Frederick Creecy, Nathan Creecy, Wm Gregory - Patroler, Jonathan Haughton, Abraham Hassell - Constable, Jesse Hassell, Richard Haughton, John Halsey, Edward Haughton, Charles Haughton, Jonathan James, John Leary, Frederick Luten, Geo: Liles, Thomas Miers, William Midleton, James Ming, Edmund Norcom, John Pettyjohn, Robert Perkins, Job Pettyjohn, Thomas Rea, James Sanders, John Simons Junr., William Simons, John Simons Senr., Thomas Taylor - Patroler, George Wilkins, Francis Wilder, Holaday Walton, Wilson Webb, Joseph Beasley - Patroler.

****

Capt. McGuire

Micajah Bunch, William Badham, John Bond Junr., John B. Bennett, Benjamin Coffield, William Eelbeck, Nathaniel Howcot, Baker Hoskins, Richard Hoskins - Patroler, Arthur Howe, Samuel Hoskins, Thomas Jones, Li[?] Jones, Zachariah Jones, James Jones, William Jones, John Luten, Mason Miller, Phillip McGuire, Thomas Mathias, Michal M. **[Smudged]**, Wilson Mewborn, Nicholas Newborn - Patroler, Abraham Norfleet, Jeremiah Price, Seth Parker, Isaac Parker, John Padjett, Reuben Small, Reuben Simons, Abraham Small, Benjamin Small, Thomas W. Thomson, John Wilder, Nathaniel Wilder, William Bennett, John Coffield - Patroler.

****

Capt Skinners

Miles Elliott, William Ford, William Gooden, John Hoskins, Malichea Halsey, Reuben Hobbs, Colen Halsey, Jeremiah Ashley, Colen Bunch, Abner Bunch, James Bond, John Brinn, Jacob Boyce, William Deal, Bond Jamison, Josiah Jones, William Jordan, Hance Jordan, Jackson Williams, Demsey Jordan, Job Leary, Samuel McGuire, John McGuire, Wm. Muns Junr., John Mitchell, William Mitchell, John Mitchell Junr., William Newborn, Willis Parker, Elisha Parker, Joseph Parish, Seth Reddick, Exum Simpson, Samuel Skinner, Richard Skinner, Samuel Topping, Richard Woodward, Isaac Welch, Edward Woodward, John Ward, John Parish, John B. Griffin, William Hix.

Chowan County
Patrol Records

****

Capt. Cullens District

Willis Griffen, Joseph Goodwin, Forehand Thomas, Cader Felton, John Felton, Wm Felton, Shadrick Felton, ~~Micajah Chapple~~, Josiah Chapple, James Chapple, Joseah Copeland, Jacob Cullens, Isaac Byram Senr., Jas. Byram, Thomas Browrigg, Exum Goodwin, Lewis Goaden, Joseph Hudson, Henry Herdle, Josiah Jordan, Joseph Jordan (son of Joe), Ichabod ~~Jordan - but he is not fit to be a Juror~~, Jacob Jordan, Joseph Jordan - Son of Jacob, Nathan Jordan, Caleb Jordan, Wm Murfree, Robert Moore, Isaac Byram, Junr., Joel Byram, John Perry, Samuel Perry Junr., ~~Samuel Parker~~, James Smith, ~~Joseph Scott Senr.~~, Miles Stallings, John **[Smudged]**, John Smith, John Twine, Nathl Taylor x moved, Shadrick Ward, Joshua White, Josiah Ward, Fredk. Ward, Humphry, ~~Jacob Ward - no freehold~~, Edward Welch, William Ward, Jeremiah Ward, John Evans, ~~James Evans~~, Jesse White.

****

State of No. Carolina   } Chowan County Court
                         } June Term 1803

Whereas by an Act passed at the last Assembly, the several County Courts are fully impowered to appoint Patrolers in their respective Counties, if Deemed necessary under such rules, regulations and instructions, as they may direct.

Ordered that one Good and Descent person be appointed in each Captains District, who shall be Designated, the Capt of the patrole of such District who shall be impowered and is hereby required to appointed immediately three good Men to act and serve under him as Patrolers.

That the Captain and patrolers shall during their continuance in office, be exempted from serving as Jurors, working on the Road, and shall be further entitled to the Sum of forty shillings, each to be paid out of the County Tax by the Sheriff, who shall be allowed for the same in the Settlement of his Accounts. That all the arms that shall be found hereafter in the hands or habitations of Slaves, without leave having first been obtained agreeable to Act of Assembly shall be seized by the said Patrolers and lodged with the

Chowan County
Patrol Records

Clerk of this Court and as information being given to the insuing Court, if the same be ordered to be sold the amount arising from the Sale shall be divided equally amongst the patrolers who shall have found and seized them after deducting 5 Pct commission to the Sheriff or other officer whom shall perform the sale.

Ordered also, that the said Patrolers appointed as aforesaid shall Patrole their respective districts once at least in two weeks or oftener if the Captain should deem it necessary for the purpose of carrying the Law respecting Servants and Slaves into effect.

And on failure or neglect to perform such services every person so failing or neglecting shall forfeit and pay the sum of forty Shillings for every delinquency, moveable before any Justice of the Peace, one half to the use of the informer and the other half to the use of the County.

It is further ordered, that the Capt only of the said patrolers shall have power to order punishment to be inflicted not exceeding fifteen lashes as all Slaves that they may find off their Owners plantation, or travelling on the Sabbath or other unreasonable times without a permit or pass of such owner or other person having the care of such Slave or Slaves.

It is further ordered, the following persons be appointed Captains, To wit.

In Capt Simons District   Solomon Elliot
In Capt Hoskins District   Richard Hoskins
In Capt Skinners District   Wm. Jackson, Junr.
In Capt Cullins District   John [?]ullington
In Edenton   Charles Roberts

And it is further ordered that the said Captains and Patroles are, and shall be appointed for the Term of twelve Months.

Ordered that the Clerk issue a Copy of the present order, and send it to the Captain of each District who is requested to have the same made at the head of his Company on the two succeeding Musters, and that the said Clerk shall also cause it to be advertised at these or more public place in the County.
Test. N. Norfleet, Clk.

****

State of North Carolina   } Chowan County Court
                                   } June Term 1803

Chowan County
Patrol Records

This Certifys that William Jackson was appointed Capt. Of the Patrole in Capt. Skinners District for the ensuing year
Allowed Settlement
Test. E Norfleet, CS

****

State of North Carolina } Chowan County Court
                                    } June Term 1803

This Certifys that John Fullington was appointed Capt. Of the Patrole in Capt. Cullins district for the ensuing year & that he appoint three men to act under him.
Allowed Settlement
Test. E Norfleet

****

State of North Carolina } Chowan County Court
                                    } June Term 1803

This Certifys that Richard Hoskins was appointed Capt of the Patrole in Capt Hoskins District for the ensuing year.
Allowed Settlement
Test. E Norfleet

****

Daniel McDowells Patrollers
Order
For Service and return to March Term 1821
Executed, J R P[?]

State of North Carolina }
Chowan County Court } December Term 1821

    Ordered, that Daniel McDowell, Wm. D Roscoe, Joseph F. Faribault, James Gorham, Thos. T Charlton and John G Hankins, be

Chowan County
Patrol Records

appointed patrollers for the Town of Edenton, to patrol at least once a week, and that Daniel McDowell be the captain
Test. Henry Wills, Clk

****

State of North Carolina }
Chowan County Court } August Term 1842

Ordered, That William Privitt Junr. Be allowed Six dollars for one years service as Patroll in the Middle District under Ephraim Goodwin Capt. And that the Sheriff pay the same when in funds and be allowed it in settlement of his Account.
$6 --Test T.V. Hathaway, Clk

****

Thomas Cockran, Capt. Of the Patroll
On the West Side of the Virginia Road
Capt. Pains District
Sept Term 1829

Executed by delivering a True Copy of this Order, Thos Cockran, 27th Oct 1829, Wm. D. Roscoe, Shff.

Rec'd payment from WD Roscue, Shff
Thomas Cochran Junr.
For Wm. Privitt Senr.

State of North Carolina }
Chowan County Court } September Term 1829

    Ordered, that Paul Bunch, Humphry Wright, Samuel Privitt, David Harrel Senr., and Thomas Cockran (as the Capt) be appointed a Patroll on the West Side of the Virginia Road Called Pains District.
Test Edm Hoskins, Clk

****

Obed Small, Capt. Of the Patroll

Chowan County Patrol Records

Green Hall District
Sept Term 1829

Executed by delivering a Copy of this Order to Obed Small, 7th Oct. 1829, Wm. D. Roscoe

State of North Carolina } September Term 1829
Chowan County Court   }

Ordered that John G Small, Samuel Chambers, Alfred Satterfield, Humphry Small, Wm. G. Leary and Obed. Small (as the Capt.) be appointed a Patroll in Green Hall district.
Test. Edm. Hoskins, Clk

****

Myles Wright Capt. Of the Patroll
In the upper District
September Term 1829

Executed by Delivering a Copy of this order to Myles Wright, 13th Oct. 1829. Test. Wm.D. Roscoe, Shff

State of North Carolina }
Chowan County Court   } September Term 1829

Ordered that Wm Bush, Joseph Hurdle, Willis Welch, Jacob Cullings, and Myles Wright, as Capt. Be appointed a Patroll in the upper District
Test. Edm. Hoskins, Clk

****

Order, Samuel Simpson
Capt. Of the Patroll
In Capt Bunch's District

Executed by leaving a Copy of this Order at the dwelling House of Saml. Simpson, 22nd Febr. 1830
Wm D. Roscoe, Shff

Chowan County
Patrol Records

State of North Carolina   } December Term 1829
Chowan County Court   }

    Ordered, that, Thomas J. Brownrigg, Cullen Bunch, Allen Small, Henderson Simpson, Everard Garrett be appointed a Patroll, on the East Side of the Virginia Road, in Capt. Bunch District, and that Samuel Simpson be appointed Captain of said Patroll, in the place of Everard Garrett.
Test. Edm. Hoskins, Clk

****

Everard Garrett, Capt. Of the Patroll
Capt. Paines Dist.
Sept. Term 1829

Executed by delivering a Copy of this Order to Everard Garrett, 12th October 1829. Wm. D. Roscoe, Shff

State of North Carolina   }
Chowan County Court   } September Term 1829

    Ordered, that Moses Bark, Timothy Evans, Henderson Simpson, Samuel Simpson, Everard Garrett (as the Capt.) be appointed a Patroll on the East Side of the Virginia Road, in the District Called Paines
Test. Edm. Hoskins, Clk

****

State of North Carolina   } Chowan County Court
                                  } June Term 1804

This Certifys that George Waff is appointed Capt. Of the Patrole for the ensuing year in the Town of Edenton.
Test. E Norfleet

George Waff   2 " 0 " 0
John Fife   2 " 0 " 0
Noah Hinten   2 -----------

Chowan County
Patrol Records

Archibald Leath   2-------------
                        8 " 0 " 0

Rec'd of Charles Roberts forty Shillings for My att[?]
George Waff

****

Leml. Skinner Capt of the Patroll below
         Edenton   } Order
       June Term 1830

Executed by delivering a Copy of this Order to Leml Skinner 3rd July 1830
Wm D Roscoe, Shff

State of North Carolina   }
Chowan County Court   } June Term 1830

       Ordered, that Lemuel Skinner Capt., Nathan Gregory, Thomas M. Carter and John Welch be appointed a Patroll in the upper part of the lower District, Called Benburys District.
Test. Edm. Hoskins, Shff

****

Jonathan H. Haughton Capt of the Patroll
Capt Benburys District

Executed by delivering a Copy of this Order to Jonathan H Haughton Esqr., 10th July 1830
Wm D. Roscoe, Shff

State of North Carolina   } Chowan County Court
                                 } June Term 1811

Ordered that Joshua S. Creecy, Lemuel Haughton, William Middleton, Allen Lasiter, Samuel Rea & Jeremiah Coffield be appointed Patrollers in Capt Haughtons Dist. For the ensuing year.
Test. E. Norfleet, Clk

Chowan County
Patrol Records

The above order was rec'd by me and directed to Mr. Wm. Middleton as Capt of the Patrols, J.S. Creecy

Rec'd 8 from 1829 from Edm. Hoskins four Dollars for attending as a Patrole last year.
William Middleton

Capt. Haughtons District. Rec'd from Edm Hoskins forty shillings for my Services as a Patroll
Leml. Haughton

Rec'd from Edm. Hoskins four dollars for my attending as a patroler
Allen Lassiter

I hereby Certify that Samuel Rea, Lemuel Haughton and Allen Lassiter Served as Patroll for one year, Middleton, Capt. Mr. Joshua S. Creecy & others Patrolers

****

Order for Patroll in the Middle District
Sep Term 1830

Executed by delivering a Copy of this Order to Hardy Hurdle this 22nd Octr. 1830.
Wm D Roscoe, Shff

State of North Carolina } September Term 1830
Chowan County Court   }

    Ordered that Myles Halsey, Richard Jordan, Paul Bunch, Benjamin Bateman and Hardy Hurdle be appointed a Patroll in the Middle District and that Hardy Hurdle be the Capt. Of Said Patroll.
Test Edm Hoskins, Clk

****

Order to Benjn White, Captain of the Patrol in the room of Charles E. Johnson. For Service, and return to Court.
Executed

Chowan County
Patrol Records

Ja. R. P[?]

State of North Carolina }
Chowan County Court } June Term 1818

    Ordered That Benjamin White be appointed Captain of the Patrol in the room of Charles E. Johnson
Test. Henry Wills, Dep. Clk.

****

To Michael Wilder for Service and Return
T December term, 1818
Executed, John Mc Cottor, Dep Shff

State of North Carolina }
Chowan County Court } September Term 1818

    Ordered, That Michael Wilder be appointed Captain of the Patrol in Capt. Blount's District, in the room of William Roberts, and that John Wilder, Lemuel C. Baines and Joseph Norcom, be Patrollers under him.
Test. Henry Wills, Dep. Clk

****

Josiah Coffield Capt. Of the Patroll
Green Hall Dist.
Decr Term 1830

Executed by delivering a Copy of this Order to Jos Coffield, 18th Febr 1831
Wm. D. Roscoe, Shff

State of North Carolina } December Term 1830
Chowan County Court }

    Ordered that Josiah Coffield, Wm. Bullock, Wm. R. Roberts and Joseph B. Skinner Esquires be appointed a Patroll for Green Hall District, and that Josiah Coffield be the Captain.
Test. Edm. Hoskins, Clk

Chowan County
Patrol Records

****

Order to John Bonner
As Capt. Of the Patrol
In Nash District

For Service and returns, March Term 1819, Copy del'd, Ja. [?]

State of North Carolina }
Chowan County Court   } December Term, 1818

     Ordered, That John Bonner be appointed Captain of the Patrol, in Captn Nash's District.
Test. Henry Wills, Dep. Clk

****

        Order for the Patroll in Green Hall Dist.
               June Term 1833

State of North Carolina } June Term 1833
Chowan County Court   }

     Ordered that Josiah Coffield, Capt. Wm. Bullock, Wm. Welch, Hardy Skinner, Humphrey Small & Nathaniel howcott be appointed a Patroll in Green Hall District.
Issued 21 June 1833
Test. Edm Hoskins, Clk

****

Order to William Roberts, Capt. Of the Patrol in Captn. Blounts District
          For Service and Return to Court
             September Term 1818

Executed, Ja.[?]

State of North Carolina }
Chowan County Court   } June Term 1818

Chowan County
Patrol Records

Ordered That William Roberts be appointed Captain of the Patrol in Captain Blount's District, with liberty to appoint such Patrollers as he may choose.
Test. Henry Wills, Dep Clk

****

Order for a Patroll in upper District
June Term 1833

Executed by delivering a Copy of this Order to Jacob Cullens, Capt. 20th July 1833
Wm. D Roscoe, Shff

State of North Carolina } June Term 1818
Chowan County Court   }

Ordered that Jacob Cullings, Capt., Wm. Bush, Wm. Hurdle, Wm. Elliot, Baker H. Welch & George F. Walton, be appointed a Patroll for the upper District.
Test. Edm Hoskins, Clk

****

To Amasa Perrin For Service
Return to December Term, 1818
Executed, John M Cottor, Dep. Shff

State of North Carolina }
Chowan County Court   } September Term 1818

Ordered, That Amasa Perrin be appointed Captain of the Patrol for the Town of Edenton, in the room of Joseph B. Skinner resigned, with authority to appoint Patrollers under him.
Test. Henry Wills, Dep, Clk

****

Order for the Patroll below Edenton
June Term 1833

Chowan County
Patrol Records

To be returned to Court

Executed by delivering a Copy of this Order to Leml. B. Halsey, Captn. 19th July 1833
Wm. D. Roscoe Shff

State of North Carolina }
Chowan County Court } June Term 1833

  Ordered that Lemuel B Halsey, Capt., Levy Scott, Lemuel M. Pettyjohn, Thomas C Whidbee, Joseph Norcom, John Norcom, Joseph B. Haughton, John Beasley, Wm. B. Roberts & Nathaniel J. Beasley be appointed a Patroll below Edenton.
Test. Edm. Hoskins, Clk

****

Henderson J. Standin, Captain of Patrol
For Service & Return to December Term 1819
Copy Del'd, Ja R. [?]

State of North Carolina }
Chowan County Court } September Term 1819

  Ordered, That Henderson J. Standin be appointed Captain of the Patrol in the Town of Edenton, and have power to choose Patrollers under him.
Test. Henry Wills, Dep. Clk

****

Order for the Patroll in the upper end of the Middle District
June Term 1833

Executed by delivering a Copy of this Order to Silas Elliot, Captn. 20th July 1833. Wm. D. Roscoe, Shff

State of North Carolina }
Chowan County Court } June Term 1833

Chowan County
Patrol Records

Ordered that Silas Elliott, Capt., Moses Bush, Martin Simpson, and Paul Bunch be appointed a Patroll in the upper end of the Middle District.
Test. Edm. Hoskins, Clk
Issued 21st June 1833

****

Willis Elliott, Captain of Patrol
For Service and return to December Term 1819
Copy Delivered
J R. Bent, Shff

State of North Carolina }
Chowan County Court } September Term 1819

Ordered That Willis Elliott be appointed Captain of the Patrol on the Virginia Road in Captn. Johnsons District, and have liberty to choose three men to Serve with him as Patrollers
Test. Henry Wills, Dep. Clk

****

Order for the Patroll in Rockakock
June Term 1833

Executed by delivering a Copy of this Order to Peter White, 19th July 1833
Wm. D. Roscoe, Shff

State of North Carolina }
Chowan County Court } September Term 1819

Ordered that Peter White, Nathaniel Bond Junr., & William Leary the Capt. Be appointed a Patroll in Rockakock District.
Issued 21st June 1833
Test. Edm Hoskins, Clk

****

William Bush, Captn. Of Patrol

Chowan County
Patrol Records

For Service and return to December Term, 1819
Copy Del'd, J. R. Bent[?]

State of North Carolina }
Chowan County Court } September Term 1819

    Ordered that William Bush be appointed Captain of the Patrol in Henry Elliotts District.
Test. Henry Wills, Dep. Clk

****

Order for the Patroll in the lower and of the Middle Dist.
June Term 1833

State of North Carolina }
Chowan County Court } June Term 1833

    Ordered that Cullen Bunch Capt., Allen Small, John G. Small and Henderson Simpson be appointed a Patrole in the lower end of the Middle District.
Issued 21st june 1833
Test. Edm. Hoskins, Clk

****

William D. Robertson, Captain of the Patrol
For Service and returned to December Term 1819
Copy Del'd, Ja. R. Bent[?]

State of North Carolina }
Chowan County Court } September Term 1819

    Ordered, That William D Robertson be appointed Captain of the Patrol on the Sandy Ridge Road in Captn. Johnsons District and be allowed to choose three men to serve with him as Patrollers.
Test. Henry Wills, Dep. Clk

****

Chowan County
Patrol Records

Order for Patroll, Nov 1834 below Towns

Executed by delivering a Copy of this Order to Charles W Mixon Esqr.
28th Novr. 1834
Wm. D. Roscoe, Shff

State of North Carolina }
Chowan County Court } Nov Term 1834

      Ordered that Leml B. Halsey, Thomas M. Carter, Delight Nixson, Jas F. Fareboult, Levy Scott and Charles W. Mixson Capt. Be appointed a Patroll below Edenton, to be called the Second Company.
Issued 29th Nov 1834
Test. Edm. Hoskins, Clk

****

John Goodwin, Patrollers Certificate
For Service and return to December Term, 1820

Executed by delivering a Copy of the within
J. R. Bush[?] Shff

State of North Carolina }
Chowan County Court } September Term 1820

      Ordered, That John Goodwin, Joseph Baines and Thomas Cockran be appointed Patroller from the Virginia Road to Perquimans Line
Test. Henry Wills, Clk

****

Jordan D. Elliott & als, Order for Patrol
To be returned to Court Nov Term 1837

Executed by delivering a True Copy of the within Order with Jordan D Elliott, June 1837. Wm. Roscoe, Shff, By Wm Bush Dep. Shff.

State of North Carolina }
Chowan County Court } August Term 1834

Chowan County
Patrol Records

     Ordered that Jordan D. Elliott Captain, Henderson Simpson, Perry Goodwin and Daniel V. Etheridge be appointed a Patrol in Capt. Smalls District
Test. T. V. Hathaway, Clk

****

     Order appointing Jno. M. Bond Capt. Of Patrol
For return to September Term 1820

Executed by delivering a copy of the within For Jas. R. Bush, Shff
T. V. Hathaway

State of North Carolina   }
Chowan County Courts   } June Term 1820

     Ordered, That John M. Bond be appointed Captain of the Patrol in Bullocks District, and that Edmund Bond, Richard Wilder, James Hindsley and Henry Satterfield from his company as a Patrol.
Test. Henry Wills, Clk

****

Order for a Patroll below Edenton
Nov Term 1834

Executed by handing a Copy of this Order to James Norcom Jr., 8th Decr. 1836
Wm. D. Roscoe, Shff

State of North Carolina   }
Chowan County Court   } November Term 1834

     Ordered that Thos. C. Whidbee, Jacob Eason, Joseph B. Haughton, William Norcom & James Norcom Junr, Captain be appointed a Patroll below Edenton called the first Company
Issued 27 Nov 1834
Test. Edm. Hoskins, Clk

Chowan County
Patrol Records

****

Francis Wilder, Captain of Patrol
To be served on him and returned, June Term 1820

Executed by delivering a Copy of this Notice
Ja. R. Bush, Shff

State of North Carolina }
Chowan County Court } March Term 1820

  Ordered, That Francis Wilder be appointed Captain of the Patrol in Bullocks District, and that Richard Wilder, James Hindsley, Henry Satterfield and John M. Bond, form his company as a Patrol.
Test. Henry Wills, Dep. Clk

****

Order for Peter White Capt

Executed by delivering a Copy of this Order to Jno Bond, one of the Parties herein named. 3rd Octr. 1835
Wm. D. Roscoe, Shff

State of North Carolina }
Chowan County Court } August Term 1835

  Ordered that Peter White, John Bond, Lemuel Prevett & John Parker be appointed a Patroll in Rockakock & that Peter White be the Capt. Issued Augt. 1835. Test. Edm. Hoskins, Clk

****

Willis Elliott, Patrollers Certificates
To Service and return to December Term, 1820

Executed by delivering a Copy of the within
Ja. R. Bush, Shff

State of North Carolina }

Chowan County
Patrol Records

Chowan County Court   } September Term, 1820

Ordered, That Willis Elliott, Uriah Hudson, Noah White and Myles Halsey, be appointed Patrollers from the Virginia Road to Chowan River.
Test. Henry Wills, Clk

****

Order for N J Beasley, Nov. 1835

Executed by delivering a Copy of this Order to Charles Creecy, 30th Decr. 1835
Wm D. Roscoe, Shff

State of North Carolina   }
Chowan County Court   } Nov Term 1835

Ordered that Charles Creecy & Nathaniel J. Beasley be appointed a Patroll below Edenton under James Norcom Capt.
Issued 11 Nov 1835
Test Edm. Hoskins, Clk

****

William Bush, Captain of Patrol
For Service and return to December Term, 1820
Executed by delivering a Copy of the within
Ja. R. Bush, Shff

State of North Carolina   }
Chowan County Court   } September Term 1820

Ordered, That William Bush be appointed Captain, and John Bush, Elisha Hurdle, Jacob Parker, Miles Wright and Joab Cullens, Patrollers under him in Capt. Henry Elliotts District.
Test. Henry Wills, Clk

****

Chowan County
Patrol Records

Order for the Patroll in the upper District
May Term 1835

Executed by delivering a True Copy of this Order to Wm. Bush Captain, 22nd May 1835
Wm. D. Roscoe, Shff

State of North Carolina }
Chowan County Court } May Term 1835

      Ordered that William Bush, George F. Walton, Hillary H. Eure, Wm. H. Elliott be appointed a Patrol (and Wm. Bush to be the Capt.) in the upper District.
Issued 21st May 1835
Test. Edm. Hoskins, Clk

****

William Simons, Captain of Patrol
For Service and return to December Term, 1820
Executed by delivering a Copy for Ja. R. Bush, Shff.
T.V. Hathaway

State of North Carolina }
Chowan County Court } September Term, 1820

      Ordered, That William Simons be appointed Captain of the Patrol in Captn. Benbury's district, and that John Baines, Benjamin Wynn, Abner Welch, William Roberts and Michael Wilder, be appointed Patrollers with him.
Test. Henry Wills, Clk

****

Patroll in Rockakock District, 1836
August Term
Executed by delivering a copy of this Notice
Wm. D. Roscoe, Shff

State of North Carolina }

Chowan County
Patrol Records

Chowan County   } August Term 1836

    Ordered that Edw T. Waff Capt, John Parker, and Lemuel Prevett, be appointed a Patroll in Rockakock District.
Issued 6th Augt. 1836
Test Edm. Hoskins, Clk

****

John C. Baines, Captain of Patrol
To be served on him and returned to June Term, 1820
Executed by delivering a Copy of the within
J. R. Bush, Shff

State of North Carolina   }
Chowan County Court   } March Term, 1820

    Ordered, That John C. Baines be appointed Captain of the Patrol in Captn Benburys District
Test. Henry Wills, Dep. Clk

****

Patroll Order
Executed by delivering a Copy of the within

State of North Carolina   }
Chowan County Court   } May Term 1835

    Ordered that Joseph Hurdle, Noah Ward, Micajah Blanchard & Timothy Ward (Joseph Hurdle to be the Capt.) be appointed a Patroll in the upper part of the upper District.
Issued 21st May 1835
Test. Edm. Hoskins, Clk

****

William Jackson's Patroll Order
To be served and returned, December Term 1821
Executed by leaving a copy For J.R. Bush, Shff

Chowan County
Patrol Records

W.D. Roscoe

State of North Carolina }
Chowan County Court } September Term 1821

Ordered That William Jackson, America Bunch, Jesse Parker, William Newbern and Stephen Skinner, be appointed Patrollers, William Jackson to be Captain from the Virginia Road to the Perquimans Line.
Test. Henry Wills, Clk

****

Patroll order in the Upper district
Augt. 1836
Executed by delivering a copy of this notice
W D Roscoe, Shff
By B Hathaway, D. Shff

State of North Carolina }
Chowan County Court } August Term 1836

Ordered, that Humphrey Ward, Elisha Bunch, Isard Winslow and Lemuel Bunch be appointed a Patroll, in the upper District, & that Humphrey Ward be the Capt.
Issued 6 August 1836
Test. Edm. Hoskins, Clk

****

I Certify that Stephen Elliott one of my Privates in Capt Bru[?]ood District serve in the year 1818 as a patroller for Decr 11th 1821 said District. Jonah Small Capt.

****

John Bonner's Patrol Order
To be served and returned to
December term 1821

Executed by Leaving a Copy of the within for J.R. Bush, Shff

Chowan County
Patrol Records

Wm. D. Rascoe

State of North Carolina }
Chowan County Court } September Term 1821

    Ordered That John Bonner, David Small, James Hinesly, Richard Wilder, Stephen Elliott and James Coffield be appointed Patrollers, John Bonner to be Captain for Capt Bullocks district
Test. Henry Wills, Clk

****

Order for the Patroll in Allen Smalls Dist., August 1836
Executed by delivering a copy of this notice
W. D. Rascoe, Shff
By [?] Hathaway, D Shff

State of North Carolina }
Chowan County Court } August Term 1836

    Ordered that Paul Bunch, Jordan D. Elliott, Moses Burk & Martin Simpson be appointed a Patroll in Smalls district on Sandy Ridge, & Martin Simpsons Capt.
Issued 6th August 1836
Test. Edm. Hoskins, Clk

****

Jacob Parker & als Patrol Order
To be served and returned to December Term 1821
Executed by leaving a copy of the within for J.R. Bush
W.D. Rascoe

State of North Carolina }
Chowan County Court } September Term 1821

    Ordered, That Jacob Parker, Benjamin White, Stephen Skinner, Charles Meredet and Cullen Bunch, be appointed Patrollers, in Capt Skinners district, from the Virginia Road to Chowan River
Test. Henry Wills, Clk

Chowan County
Patrol Records

****

Henry Smith & als, Order for Patrol
To be returned to Court Novr. Term 1837

Executed by delivering a Copy of this Order to Henry Smith, 18th Aug 1837
Wm.D, Rascoe, Shff

State of North Carolina }
Chowan County Court } August Term 1837

    Ordered, That Henry Smith Captain, Alfred Smith, Saml. Chambers, Wm G. Liles & Henry Whidbee appointed a Patrol in Green Hall District
Test. T. V. Hathaway, Clk

****

John Boyce Patrol, Certificate
To serve and return to March Term 1823
Executed by delivering a Copy of the notice
J.R. Bush, Shff

State of North Carolina }
Chowan County Court } December Term 1822

    Ordered That, John Boyce be appointed Patroler in Captain Skinners district in the room of Henderson Simpson
Test. Henry Wills, Clk

****

Henry Smith & als, Order for Patrol
To be left with Henry Smith Capt.

State of North Carolina }
Chowan County Court } August Term 1837

Chowan County
Patrol Records

Ordered that Henry Smith Captain, Alfred Smith, Saml. P. Chambers, William G. Liles & Henry W. Hobbs be appointed a patrol in Green Hall District.
Test. T.V. Hathaway, Clk

****

Charles Haughton's Patroll, Order
For service and return to June Term 1822
Executed by leaving a true Copy of the within with Charles Haughton
For J R Bush, Shff
Wm D Rascoe

State of North Carolina }
Chowan County Court } March Term 1822

Ordered, That Charles Haughton, Mackey Gregory, Joseph Norcom, Lemuel Hoskins, Joseph Hoskins and William Benbury, be appointed Patrollers in Captain Benbury's District, Charles Haughton to be the Captain.
Test. Henry Wills, Clk

****

Miles Wright et als, Patroll order
To be returned to November Term 1838
Executed by delivering a Copy of this Notice to Miles Wright
1st Octr. 1838, W.D. Rascoe, Shff
By Wm. Bush

State of North Carolina }
Chowan County Court } August Term 1838

Ordered that Miles Wright, Robert Creecy, Matthew Baker, William Jackson, and Willis Welch be appointed Patroll, in the Upper District, and that Miles Wright be Captain.
Issued 30th August 1838
Test. John Bush, Clk
By T.V. Hathaway, D. Clk

Chowan County
Patrol Records

****

James Rawls and others, Patroll Order
For Service and return to December Term 1822
Executed, J. R. Bush, Shff

State of North Carolina }
Chowan County Court } September Term 1822

  Ordered, That James Rawls, James Binum and William Bush be appointed Patrollers in the lower part of Henry Elliotts District, James Rawls to be Captain.
Test. Henry Wills, Clk

****

Silas W. Elliott et als, Patroll Order
To be returned to November term 1838
Executed by delivering a Copy of this order
To Silas W Elliott, 1st Octr. 1838
W D Rascoe, Shff
By Wm Bush

State of North Carolina }
Chowan County Court } August Term 1838

  Ordered, that Silas W. Elliott, Theophilus White & Richard Simpson be appointed Patroll in the Middle District in Bear Swamp and that Silas W. Elliott be Captain
Issued 30th August 1838
Test John Bush, Clk
By T.V. Hathaway, D. Clk

****

Miles Elliott & others, Patrollers Order
For Service and return to December Term 1822
Executed, J.R. Bush, Shff

State of North Carolina }

Chowan County
Patrol Records

Chowan County Court } September Term 1822

    Ordered, that Miles Elliott, James Brinn, Henderson Simpson, Jesse Parker, and Paul Bunch, be appointed Patrollers from the Virginia Road to the Perquimans Line, Miles Elliott to be Captain
Test. Henry Wills, Clk

****

Patroll Order for Thos. Bogue Capt. Et al
To be returned to August Term 1838, 26th May
Executed by delivering a Copy of this Order to Tho. Bogue
26th May 1838
W.D. Rascoe, Shff

State of North Carolina }
Chowan County Court } May Term 1838

    Ordered, that Thomas Bogue, Elisha Bunch, Humphrey Ward, Noah Ward, and Timothy Ward be appointed Patroll for the upper part of the Upper District above William Bush's and that Thomas Bogue be Captain.
Issued 22nd May 1838
Test. John Bush, Clk
By T.V. Hathaway, D. Clk

****

Jacob Parkers Patrollers, Order
For Service and return to June Term 1822
Executed by leaving a True copy of the within
With Jacob Parker
For J. R. Bush, Shff
Wm. D. Rascoe

State of North Carolina }
Chowan County Court } March Term, 1822

Chowan County
Patrol Records

Ordered, That Jacob Parker, Benjamin White, Cullen Bunch, James Roberts and Noah White, be appointed Patrollers in Captain Skinners District from the Virginia Road to Chowan River.
Test. Henry Wills, Clk

****

Order for Patroll in Sandyridge district
To be returned to May Term 1838
Executed by delivering a Copy of the within
To John G Small, 3rd March 1838
Wm. D. Rascoe, Shff

State of North Carolina }
Chowan County Court } February Term 1838

Ordered that John G. Small, John R. Jordan and Baker Small be appointed Patroll in Sandy ridge district and that John G. Small be Captain. Issued 20th Feby 1838
Test. T.V. Hathaway, D. Clk

****

Jacob Parker Junr., & others, Patrollers Order
For Service and Return to December Term, 1822
Executed
J. R. Bush, Shff

State of North Carolina }
Chowan County Court } September Term 1822

Ordered, That Jacob Parker, Junr., Miles Wright and Josiah Cullens, be appointed Patrollers in the upper part of Henry Elliotts District, Jacob Parker Junr., to be Captain.
Test. Henry Wills, Clk

****

Order for Patroll in the Middle District
To be returned to May Term 1838

Chowan County
Patrol Records

Executed by delivering a Copy of this Order to James Roberts
Wm. D. Rascoe, Shff
By Wm. Bush

State of North Carolina }
Chowan County Court } February Term 1838

Ordered, that James Roberts, Paul Bunch, Ephraim Goodwin, John Churchill and William Roberts be appointed Patroll in the Middle district and that James Roberts be Captain.
Issued 20th Feby 1838
Test. John Bush, Clk
By T.V. Hathaway, Dep. Clk

****

William Bullock & others, Patrollers Orders
For Service and Return to December Term, 1822
Executed, J. R. Bush, Shff

State of North Carolina }
Chowan County Court } September Term 1822

Ordered, That William Bullock, Josiah Small, Obed Small, Jeremiah Newborn. Eden Bond and Thomas Satterfield, be appointed Patrollers in Capt Bullocks District, William Bullock to be Captain of the Patrol.
Test. Henry Wills, Clk

****

Patroll Order for Thomas Bogue et al
To be left with Thomas Bogue, Captain

State of North Carolina }
Chowan County Court } May Term 1838

Ordered, that Thomas Bogue, Elisha Bunch, Humphrey Ward, Noah Ward, and Timothy Ward, be appointed Patroll for the Upper part of the Upper District above William Bush's and that Thomas Bogue be Captain.

Chowan County
Patrol Records

Issued 22nd May 1838
Test. John Bush, Clk
By T.V. Hathaway, D. Clk

****

Thomas Wilder, Patroller
To be served and returned to Sept Term 1823
Executed by delivering a Copy
J.R. Bush, Shff

State of North Carolina }
Chowan County Court } June Term 1823

     Ordered, that Thomas Wilder be appointed a Patroller in Captn James Howcotts District for the ensuing year in addition to those appointed at March Term last
Test. Henry Wills, Clk

****

Order for Patroll in the District below Edenton
To be returned to May Term 1838
Executed by delivering a Copy of the within Order
To John Leary, Capt., 27th Feb 1838
Wm. D. Rascoe, Shff

State of North Carolina }
Chowan County Court } February Term 1838

     Ordered that John H. Leary, Joshua Skinner and Thomas G. Haughton be appointed Patroll in the district below Edenton and that John H. Leary be Captain.
Issued 20th Feby 1838
Test. John Bush, Clk
By T.V. Hathaway, Dep. Clk

****

Order to Thomas Whedbee, Captain of Patrol

Chowan County
Patrol Records

For Service and Return to June Term 1823
Executed and left a True copy of this Notice
James R. Bush, Shff
By Wm D Rascoe

State of North Carolina }
Chowan County Court } March Term 1823

    Ordered, That Thomas Whedbee, John C. Baines, Robert Bartee, William C. Roberts and Wiley Everitt, be appointed Patrollers in Captain Howcott's District, Thomas Whedbee to be Captain, and that each of them take the oath prescribed by law.
Test. Henry Wills, Clk

****

Order for Patroll in the Upper district from Ballards Bridge to Wm Bush's
To be returned to May Term 1838
Executed by delivering a Copy of this Order to Jacob N Parker, Capt
24th Febr. 1838
Wm. D. Rascoe, Shff

State of North Carolina }
Chowan County Court } February Term 1838

    Ordered that Jacob N Parker, Baker F. Welch, William H. Elliott, Jacob Cullens and William Jackson be appointed Patroll from Ballards Bridge to William Bush's and that Jacob N. Parker be Captain.
Issued 20th Feby 1838
Test. John Bush, Clk
By T.V. Hathaway, Dep Clk

****

William R. Norcom's Order for Patrol
For Service and return to March Term 1824
J.R. Bush, Shff

State of North Carolina }
Chowan County Court } December Term 1823

Chowan County
Patrol Records

Ordered, That William R Norcom, Edward Waff, Lemuel Skinner, William Grimes & Samuel T Sawyer be appointed Patrollers in the Town of Edenton, William R Norcom to be Captain, and that they be directed to Patrol the Town once a Week, or oftener if they think proper, under the Penalty of One Dollar for each neglect.

****

Alex Spence et als, Patroll order
To be returned to November Term 1838

State of North Carolina }
Chowan County Court } August Term 1838

Ordered, that Alexander Spence, Charles R. Howcott, Henry W. Hobbs, Edwin Evans and Alfred Smith be appointed a Patroll in the Green Hall District and that Alexander Spence be Captain.
Issued 30th August 1838
Test. John Bush, Clk
By T.V. Hathaway, Dep. Clk

****

James Coffield, Captain, Patrol order
For Service and return to March Term 1824
Copy delivered
J.R. Bush, Shff

State of North Carolina }
Chowan County Court } December Term 1823

Ordered, That James Coffield, Josiah Coffield, Allen Jones, Obed Small, David Small & Thomas Simons, be Appointed Patrollers in Green Hall District, James Coffield to be Captain.
Test. Henry Wills, Clk

****

Fredk. L. Roberts et als, order for Patrol

Chowan County
Patrol Records

To be returned to February Term 1839
Executed by delivering a Copy of the within Order
To Fred. L. Roberts 15th Novr 1838
W.D. Rascoe, Shff

State of North Carolina }
Chowan County Court } November Term 1838

    Ordered, That Frederick L. Roberts, George W. Bruer, Thomas W. Hudgins, William Rea, James C. Bond and Charles C. Taber be appointed a Patrol in the Town of Edenton, and that Frederick L. Roberts be Captain.
Issued 13th Nov 1838
Test. John Bush, Clk
By T.V. Hathaway, Dep. Clk

****

Jas Roberts & others, Patrol Order
To be left with Jas Roberts Captain
Ephraim Goodwin, Santford E. Goodwin
Henry Hurdle, James Robertson, Thos Cockran

State of North Carolina }
Chowan County Court } February Term 1839

    Ordered That James Roberts, Paul Bunch, Ephraim Goodwin, John Churchill, and William Roberts be appointed Patroll in the Middle District and that James Roberts be Captain.
Issued 9th March 1839
Test. John Bush, Clk
By T.V. Hathaway, Dep. Clk

****

Elisha Bunch and others, Patroll Order
To be returned to August Term 1839
Executed by delivering a Copy of this Order to
Elisha Bunch, 10th June 1839
W.D. Rascoe, Shff

Chowan County
Patrol Records

By Wm Bush D Shff

State of North Carolina }
Chowan County Court } May Term 1839

Ordered, That Elisha Bunch, Thomas Bogue, Robert Hurdle, Lemuel Hurdle and William Hurdle, be appointed Patroll in the upper District and that Elisha Bunch be Captain
Issued 20th May 1839
Test. John Bush, Clk
By T.V. Hathaway, D. Clk

****

To be left with Edmd Brink by Capt of Patrol
In Capt Skinners District
Executed by leaving a copy of the Order
Wm D Rascoe
For James R. Bush, Shff

State of North Carolina }
Chowan County Court } December term 1823

Ordered, That the Patrollers in each Captains District in the County be directed to turn out once in every week, (and Sundays if necessary) during one year, and oftener if they think proper and are called out by the Captain, under the penalty of one dollar for each neglect.
Test. Henry Wills, Clk

****

To be left with James Coffield, Capt of Patrol in Bullocks District
Executed by leaving a copy of this order
James R. Bush, Shff
By Wm D Rascoe, D. Shff

State of North Carolina }
Chowan County Court } December Term 1823

Chowan County
Patrol Records

Ordered, That the Patrollers in each Captns. District in the County be directed to turn out once in every Week & Sundays if necessary, during one Year & oftener if they think proper & are called out by the Captain under the Penalty of One Dollar for each neglect.
Test. Henry Wills, Clk

****

Willis Small's Patrollers Order
To be served on him and returned
December Term 1823
Left Copy of this order
James R Bush, Shff
By Wm D. Rascoe

State of North Carolina }
Chowan County Court   } September Term 1823

Ordered, that Willis Small, James Brinn, Henderson Simpson, Jesse Parker and Paul Bunch be appointed Patrollers from the Virginia Road to the Perquimans Line, Willis Small to be Captain.
Test. Henry Wills, Clk

****

Jas Roberts & others, Patrol order
To be returned to May term 1839

Executed 12th March 1839 by delivering a Coppy of the within notice for
W.D. Roscoe, Shff
R.W. Hathaway, D. Shff

State of North Carolina }
Chowan County Court   } February Term 1839

Ordered, That James Roberts, Paul Bunch, Ephraim Goodwin, John Churchill and William Roberts be appointed Patroll in the Middle District and that James Roberts be Captain.
Issued 9th March 1839
Test. John Bush, Clk

Chowan County
Patrol Records

By T.V. Hathaway, D. Clk

****

William Coffield, Captain of Patrol's Order
For Service and return to March Term 1824
Copy Del'd
J.R. Bush, Shff

State of North Carolina }
Chowan County Court } December Term 1824

    Ordered, That William Coffield, John Bonner, Henderson Jones, Edmund Bond, David Small and William Welch be appointed Patrollers in Green Hall District, William Coffield to be the Captain
Test. Henry Wills, Clk

****

Samuel Eshon & others, Patrol Order
To be returned to November Term 1839

Executed by delivering a Copy of this Order to Saml. Eshon, 24th August 1839
W.D. Rascoe, Shff

State of North Carolina }
Chowan County Court } August Term 1839

    Ordered, That Samuel Eshon, Silas W. Elliott, John Bond, John Bouner and Edwin Evans, be appointed patrols in Captain Smiths Districts, and that Samuel Eshon be Captain.
Issued 21st August 1839
Test. John Bush, Clk
By T.V. Hathaway, D. Clk

****

Edmund Brinkley, Captain of Patrol
For Service and return to March Term 1824

Chowan County
Patrol Records

Copy delivered
J. R. Bush, Shff

State of North Carolina }
Chowan County Court } December Term 1824

    Ordered, That Edmund Brinkley, Nathan Parish, Thomas Cockran, Jeremiah Newborn & Jesse Bunch, be appointed Patrolers, in Captain Skinner's District, Edm Brinkley to be Captain.
Test Henry Wills, Clk

****

George L. Hathaway & others
Patrol order for the lower part of the District below Edenton
To be returned to November Term 1840

Executed by delivering a Copy of this Order to George L. Hathaway, 12th Sept 1840
W.D. Rascoe, Shff

State of North Carolina }
Chowan County Court } August Term 1840

    Ordered, That Thomas Hoskins, George L. Hathaway, Nathaniel J. Beasley and Lemuel Leary be appointed an additional Patrol in the District below Edenton for the lower part, and that George L. Hathaway be Captain
Issued 24th August 1840
Test. John Bush, Clk
By T.V. Hathaway, D. Clk

****

Thomas Waff Order for Patrol
For Service and return to March Term 1825
Copy Delivd.
J. R. Bush, Clk

State of North Carolina }

Chowan County
Patrol Records

Chowan County Court   } December Term 1824

    Ordered That William D. Rascoe, William Grimes, John G. Hankins and Samuel Charlton, be added to the Patrol in the Town of Edenton, and that Thomas Waff be the Captain of the said Patrol.
Test. Henry Wills, Clk

****

Patrol Order for Middle District
Ephraim Goodwin, Capt.
To be returned to November Term 1840

Executed by delivering a Copy of this order to Ephraim Goodwin, 14th Augt. 1840
W.D. Rascoe, Shff
By Geo.M Williams, D.Shff

State of North Carolina   }
Chowan County Court   } August Term 1840

    Ordered, that Ephraim Goodwin, Sandford E. Goodwin, Henry Hurdle, James Robertson Junr., amd Thomas Cockrain Junr., be appointed Patroll in the Middle District, and that Ephraim Goodwin be Captain.
Issued 14th August 1840
Test. John Bush, Clk
By T.V. Hathaway, D. Clk

****

Samuel Simpson, Captn. Of Patrol
For Service and return to December Term 1824
Executed by delivering a Copy of this Notice
J.R. Bush, Shff

State of North Carolina   }
Chowan County Court   } September Term 1824

Chowan County
Patrol Records

Ordered, That Samuel Simpson, William Newborne, Jeremiah and Lemuel Garrett, be appointed Patrollers in Captn. Skinners District; and that Samuel Simpson be Captain.
Test. Henry Wills, Clk

****

Patrol Order for additional Patrol on James Norcom Junr., Patrol
To be returned to November Term 1840

Executed by delivering a Copy of this Order to James Norcom, Jr., 10th Sept. 1840
W.D. Rascoe, Shff
By T.V. Hathaway, DS

State of North Carolina }
Chowan County Court } August Term 1840

Ordered, That William B. Hathaway & Frederick C. Gregory be appointed Patrol on the Patrol of which James Norcom Junr. Is Captain in place of Nathaniel J Beasley who has been placed upon another Patrol, & in place of Townsend Wright who has removed to Edenton.
Issued 24th August 1840
Test. John Bush, Clk
By T.V. Hathaway, D. Clk

****

Samuel Simpson, Capt. Of Patrol
For Service and return to December Term 1824
Executed by delivering a Copy of this Notice
J.R. Bush, Shff

State of North Carolina }
Chowan County Court } September Term 1824

Ordered, That Samuel Simpson, William Newborn, Jeremiah Newborn and Lemuel Garrett, be appointed Patrollers in Capt. Skinners District, and that same Simpson be Captain.
Test. Henry Wills, Clk

Chowan County
Patrol Records

****

William R. Norcom, Captain of Patrol
For Service and return to September Term 1824
A Copy Delivered
J.R. Bush, Shff

State of North Carolina }
Chowan County Court } June Term 1824

Ordered, That Joseph F. Tanbault, George Blair Junr., Thomas M. Blount and Thomas Waff, be added to the Patrol in Edenton, over which William R. Norcom is Captain.
Test. Henry Wills, Clk

****

Patrol order for Patrol in Edenton for Wm Rea & others
To be Returned to November Term 1840

Executed by delivering a Copy of this Order to Wm. Rea 25th August 1840
W.D. Rascoe, Shff

State of North Carolina }
Chowan County Court } August Term 1840

Ordered, That William Rea, Willis J. Elliott, Isaiah Kerby and James Cogan be appointed Patrol in and for the Town of Edenton, and that William Rea be Captain
Issued 24th August 1840
Test. John Bush, Clk
By T.V. Hathaway, D. Clk

****

Order to be served on John H. Leary
Returned to September Term 1824
A Copy delivered.
J.R. Bush, Shff

Chowan County
Patrol Records

State of North Carolina   }
Chowan County Court   } June Term 1824

    Ordered, That Josiah McKeel be exempt from serving as a Patrol in Captain Howcotts's District, and that Joseph Jackson be appointed in his stead; John H. Leary to be Captain of the Patrol.
Test. Henry Wills, Clk

****

Josiah McKeel, Captain of Patrols Order
For Service and return to June Term 1824
A Copy delivered
J.R. Bush, Shff

State of North Carolina   }
Chowan County Court   } March Term 1824

    Ordered, That Josiah McKeel, Edmund Benbury, John Leary, Delight Nixon, Thomas Leary and Thomas Gregory be appointed Patrollers in Captn. Howcott's District; Josiah McKeel to be Captain.
Test. Henry Wills, Clk

****

Patroll Order for Noah Ward & others
To be returned to August Term 1840

Executed by delivering a Copy of this Order to Noah Ward, 31st May 1840
W.D. Rascoe, Shff
By Wm. Bush

State of North Carolina   }
Chowan County Court   } May Term 1840

    Ordered, That Noah Ward, Lemuel Hurdle, Elisha Bunch, Thomas Bogue and Jacob Spivey be appointed Patroll in the Upper District, and that Noah ward be Captain.
Issued 22nd May 1840

Chowan County
Patrol Records

Test John Bush, Clk
By T.V. Hathaway, D Clk

****

August Term 1842

Ordered that the following persons be appointed a Patroll in Rockakock R.R. Felton Captain, Chas Smith, Wm L Smith, Stack Perry & Jer. Smith.

****

Willis Small, Captain of Patrol's Order
For Service and return to June Term 1824
Copy Delivered
J.R. Bush, Shff

State of North Carolina }
Chowan County Court } March Term 1824

    Ordered, That Willis Small, Jesse Parker, Paul Bunch, Willis Ellis and William Lane be appointed Patrollers in Captn Skinners District; Willis Small to be Captain
Test. Henry Wills, Clk

****

Jacob Parker, Captain of Patrol Order
For Service and return to June Term 1824
Copy Delivered
J.R. Bush, Shff

State of North Carolina }
Chowan County Court } March Term 1824

    Ordered, That Jacob Parker, Jacob Cullens Junr., Timothy Trotsman, Humphrey White, James Biram, William Moore, Timothy Ward, John Bush and Hardy Hurdle be appointed Patrollers in the Upper District; Jacob Parker to be Captain.
Test. Henry Wills, Clk

Chowan County
Patrol Records

****

Thomas Bogue et als, Patrol Order
To be left with Thomas Bogue, Captain

State of North Carolina }
Chowan County Court } November Term 1842

Ordered, That Thomas Bogue, Jacob Spivey, Lemuel Hurdle and Noah Ward, be appointed a Patroll in the Upper District, and that Thomas Bogue be Captain.
Issued 5th Decr 1842
Teste T.V. Hathaway, Clk

****

John Boyce's Order for Patrol
For Service and return to September Term 1826
Executed by del'd a Copy of the within
Wm. D. Rascoe, Shff
By T.V. Hathaway, DS

State of North Carolina }
Chowan County Court } June Term 1826

Ordered, That John Boyce, Edmund Bunch, Samuel Simpson, Baker Boyce and William Dail, be appointed Patrollers for Rockakock District east of the Virginia Road; John Boyce to be Captain
Test. Henry Wills, Clk

****

Ephraim Goodwin & others, Patrol Order
To be left with Ephraim Goodwin, Capt.

State of North Carolina }
Chowan County Court } August Term 1842

Chowan County
Patrol Records

    Ordered, that Ephraim Goodwin, Henry Hurdle, James Robertson, Thomas Cockrain Junr., and William Privitt Junr., be appointed a Patroll in the Middle District, and that Ephraim Goodwin be Captain.
Issued 16th August 1842
Test. T.V. Hathaway, Clk

****

James Rea, Captn Patrol
For Service and return to March Term 1826
Executed by delivering a copy of this Notice to James Rea
This 30th Decr 1826
Wm D Rascoe, Shff

State of North Carolina   }
Chowan County Court   } December Term 1826

    Ordered, That James Rea, Thomas Benbury, Samuel Halsey and Joseph N. Hoskins, be appointed Patrollers in the Lower District; James Rea to be Captain
Test Henry Wills, Clk

****

Robert R. Felton & others, Patrol order
To be left with Robert R. Felton, Capt.

State of North Carolina   }
Chowan County Court   } August Term 1842

    Ordered, that Robert R. Felton, Charles Smith, William L. Smith, Jeremiah Smith and Starkey Perry, be appointed a Patroll in the District of Rockahock, and that Robert R. Felton be Captain.
Issued 16th August 1842
Test. T.V. Hathaway, Clk

****

John Bonners Order for Patrol
For Service and returned to September Term 1826

Chowan County
Patrol Records

Executed by del'd a Copy
Wm D. Rascoe, Shff
By T.V. Hathaway

State of North Carolina }
Chowan County Court } June Term 1826

      Ordered, That John Bonner, Abraham Alphin, Henry Satterfield, Edmund Bond, John Mann and James Hinesby, be appointed Patrollers in Captain Satterfield's District; John Bonner to be Captain.
Test Henry Wills, Clk

****

William A Littlejohn et als, Patrol order
To be left with Wm. A. Littlejohn, Captain
Executed by delivering a Copy of this order to Wm. Littlejohn
WD Rascoe, Shff

State of North Carolina }
Chowan County Court } November Term 1842

      Ordered, That William A. Littlejohn, Frederick L. Roberts, Henry E. Rascoe, Edmund C. Blount and Frederick C. Gregory be appointed the Patroll for part of the District below Edenton and, that Wm. A. Littlejohn be Captain.
Issued 5th Decr 1842
Test T.V. Hathaway, Clk

****

Henderson D. Jones, Captain Patrol
For Service and return to March Term 1826
Executed by delivering a copy of the within
To Henderson D. Jones, Dec. 27th 1826
Wm D Rascoe, Shff

State of North Carolina }
Chowan County Court } December Term 1826

Chowan County Patrol Records

Ordered, That Henderson D. Jones be appointed Captain of the Patrol in Captn. Satterfields District, in the room of John Bonner resigned.
Test. Henry Wills., Clk

****

Ephraim Goodwin & others, Patrol Order
To be returned to November Term 1842
Executed by delivering the order the 23rd day of August 1842
W D Rascoe, Shff
By Wm Deanes, Dep. Shff

State of North Carolina }
Chowan County Court } August Term 1842

  Ordered, that Ephraim Goodwin, Henry Hurdle, James Robertson, Thomas Cochrain Junr., and William Privitt Junr., be appointed a Patroll in the Middle District, and that Ephraim be Captain.
Issued 16th August 1842
Test T.V. Hathaway, Clk

****

John Paine's Order for Patrol
For Service and return to September Term 1826
Executed by del'd a Copy of the within
Wm D Rascoe, Shff
By T.V. Hathaway, DS

State of North Carolina }
Chowan County Court } June Term 1826

  Ordered, that John Paine, Myles Halsey, Solomon Burrus, Cullen Jones, Samuel Privitt and John Parker, be appointed Patrollers for Rockahock District west of the Virginia Road; John Paine to be Captain
Test. Henry Wills, Clk

****

Joseph H. Skinner's Order for Patrol

Chowan County
Patrol Records

For Service and return to September Term 1826
Executed by del'd a Copy of the within order
Wm. D. Rascoe, Shff
By T.V. Hathaway, DS

State of North Carolina }
Chowan County Court } June Term 1826

   Ordered, that Joseph H. Skinner, James Harrell, Thomas Gregory, L.B. Lynch, Nathan Gregory and Benjamin Wynns, be appointed Patrollers in Capt. Benbury's District, Joseph H. Skinner to be Captain
Test. Henry Wills, Clk

****

   Ephraim Goodwin & others Patroll order

Ordered that the Within named persons be allowed each $4 for the last Years Services. Tho J charlton for the Const. To be left with E. Goodwin, Capt.

State of North Carolina }
Chowan County Court } June Term 1843

   Ordered, That Ephraim Goodwin, Joseph B. Newby, James Robertson, Thomas Cochrain Junr., and William Privitt Junr., be appointed a patroll for the Middle District and that Ephraim Goodwin be Captain. Issued Augst. 22nd 1843
Test. T.V. Hathaway, Clk

****

   William Grime's Order for Patrol
For Service and return to September Term 1826
Executed by delivering a copy
Wm. D. Rascoe, Shff
By T.V. Hathaway, DS

State of North Carolina }
Chowan County Court } June Term 1826

Chowan County
Patrol Records

Ordered, that William Grimes, William Lamb, Alexander Spence, Joseph Blount and Joseph F. Faribault be appointed Patrollers for the Town of Edenton, William Grimes to be Captain.

Ordered, That the Patrollers for the Town of Edenton, appointed appointed at this term, as well as those hereafter to be appointed, be directed to patrol the Town once a week, or oftener, if required by the Captain, under the penalty of one Dollar for each neglect.
Test. Henry Wills, Clk

****

Baker F. Welch & others Patroll order
To Be returned to November Term 1843
Executed by delivering a Coppy of the within
WD Rascoe, Shff
By Wm Deanes, Dep Shff

State of North Carolina   }
Chowan County Court   } August Term 1843

Ordered, That Baker F. Welch, James J. Cannon, Myles D. Welch, Miles Wright, William H. Elliott, and Henry Cannon, be appointed a patroll for the Upper District, and, that Baker F. Welch be Captain.
Issued Augst 1843
Test T.V. Hathaway, Clk

****

William Grime's Patroll Order
For Service and return to September Term 1827
Delivered a Copy of this Order to Wm Grimes
18th June 1827
Wm D Rascoe, Shff

State of North Carolina   }
Chowan County Court   } June Term 1827

Ordered, That William Grimes, Alexander Cheshire, William Lamb, Nathaniel Beasley, William McNider and James McNider, be

Chowan County
Patrol Records

appointed Patroller for the Town of Edenton, William Grimes to be Captain.
Test. Henry Wills, Clk

****

Patroll in Edenton
Delivered a Copy to Joseph F. Faribault
16th Septr 1828
Wm D. Rascoe, Shff
Wm. F. Bennett

State of North Carolina }
Chowan County Court } Septr. Term 1828

  Ordered, that Joseph F. Faribault, Thomas Waff, Alexander Spence, James Wills, William McNider & William Grimes be appointed a Patroll, for the Town of Edenton and that Joseph F Faribault be appointed Captain of said Patrol
Issued 16th Septr 1828
Test. Edm. Hoskins, Clk

****

Ephraim B. Elliott & others
Patroll Order
To be returned to November term 1844
Executed by leaving a copy of the within
With Ephraim B. Elliott, Sept. 13th 1844
T.S. Hoskins, Shff

State of North Carolina }
Chowan County Court } August Term 1844

  Ordered, that Ephraim B. Elliott, Miles Wright, Henry Cannon, Benjamin Gregory and Charles Hurdle, be appointed a Patrol in the Upper District, and that Ephraim B. Elliott be the Captain.
Issued 19th Augst 1844
Test. T.V. Hathaway, Clk

Chowan County
Patrol Records

****

D. McDowell Capt. Of the Patroll in Edenton
Septr Term 1829
Executed by delivering a Copy of this Order to D. McDowell
26th Octr. 1829
Wm. D. Rascoe, Shff

State of North Carolina   }
Chowan County Court   } September Term 1829

    Ordered that William Grimes, William G.H. Lamb, George Waff, Nathaniel Beasley and Daniel McDowell, as Capt. Be appointed a Patroll in the Town of Edenton for one Year.
Test. Edm. Hoskins, Clk

****

Miles Goodwin & others, Patrol Order
To be returned to November Term 1844
Executed by leaving a Copy of the within with
Miles Goodwin, Sept. 13th 1844
T.S. Hoskins, Shff

State of North Carolina   }
Chowan County Court   } August Term 1844

    Ordered that Miles Goodwin, Thomas Evans, Joseph B. Newby, Richard Goodwin, William Privitt Junr., and Thomas Cochrain Junr., be appointed a Patrol in the Middle District and that Miles Goodwin be Captain.
Issued 19th Augst 1844
Test. T.V. Hathaway, Clk

****

Capt. Paine
For Service and return to December Term 1826
Executed by delivering a Copy
Wm. D. Rascoe, Shff

Chowan County
Patrol Records

By T.V. Hathaway, DS

State of North Carolina }
Chowan County Court } September Term 1826

    Ordered, That Thomas Satterfield and Edward Waff, be appointed Patrollers in Captn. Paines Company instead of Cullen Jones and Solomon Burrus
Test. Henry Wills, Clk

****

Robert R. Felton & others, Patrol Order
To be left with Robert R. Felton, Captain

State of North Carolina }
Chowan County Court } May Term 1844

    Ordered, that Robert R. Felton, Joseph J. Bynum, John W. Hudson, Thomas Boyce and Henry Boyce be appointed a Patrol in the Rockahock District and that Robert R. Felton be Captain.
Issued 27th May 1844
Test. T.V. Hathaway, Clk

****

Patrole's Order for James Bunch, 1847
May Term 1848
No. 10.000

State of North Carolina }
Chowan County Court } May Term 1848

    Ordered that Charles Bunch be allowed the Sum of Twenty Dollars for one years Services as patroll in the bouf[?] Neck District under Samuel Eshon the Captain, and that the Sheriff pay the same, and he be allowed the same in settlement of his accounts. $20.00
Test. A. B. C. D., Clk
By E. F. G. H., Dep Clk

Chowan County
Patrol Records

****

No 354
James Boyce for Noah Ward

State of North Carolina }
Chowan County Court } November Term 1843

    Ordered, That Noah Ward be allowed four Dollars for one years services as a Patroll in the Upper District, under Thos. Bogue Captain and that the Sheriff pay the same when in funds and be allowed the same in settlement of his Account. $4
Test. T.V. Hathaway, Clk

****

No 352
Thos Bougue

State of North Carolina }
Chowan County Court } November Term 1843

    Ordered, That Thomas Bogue be allowed Four Dollars for One years Services as a Patroll in the Upper District ending this term, and that the Sheriff pay the same when in funds and be allowed in settlement of his Accounts. $4
Issued 12th decr 1843
Test T.V. Hathaway, Clk

****

State of North Carolina }
Chowan County Court } Feby Term 1848

    Ordered that Charles Smith be allowed the Sum of Twenty Dollars for one years Services as Patroll in the **[Blank]** District, under Bartemious Nixon the Capt. Of said Patroll and that the Sheriff pay the same and he be allowed it in Settlement of his afsd &c

****

Chowan County
Patrol Records

Patrol Order For Leml. Hurdle & others
Nov Term 1861
Executed by a Copy left with Leml. Hurdle
Aug 22nd 1861
P F White, Shff

State of North Carolina }
Chowan County } August Term 1861

  Ordered that Lemuel Hurdle, Riddick Hurdle, Richard Hurdle, Quenten Hurdle, Annanias Nixon and Job Winslow, be and they are appointed a Patrol for their portion of the upper District, and that said Lemuel Hurdle act as Captain thereof
Wm R Skinner, Clk

****

To Captn. Wright, Patrollers appointed
For Service and return to December Term 1826
Executed by delivering a copy of this Notice
To Miles Wright
Wm D Rascoe, Shff
Leml. [?]

State of North Carolina }
Chowan County Court } September Term 1826

  Ordered, That Hardy Hurdle, Josiah Chappel, Joseph Hurdle, Timothy Ward, Joseph Winslow and William Bush, be appointed Patrollers for Captn. Wright's District.
Test. Henry Wills, Clk

****

John Bond & others, Patrol Order
To be returned to February Term 1845
Executed by delivering a copy of the within
To John Bond, Capt., Nov. 30th 1844
T.S. Hoskins, Shff

Chowan County
Patrol Records

State of North Carolina }
Chowan County Court } November Term 1844

    Ordered, that John Bond, Samuel Eshon, Elijah Smith and Edwin Evans be appointed a Patrol in the Green Hall District and that John Bond be Captain.
Issued 15th Nov 1844
Test. T.V. Hathaway, Clk

****

Edward Garretts Order for Patrol
For Service and return to September Term 1827
Executed by delivering a copy of this Order
To E. Garrett, 12th July 1827
Wm. D. Rascoe, Shff

State of North Carolina }
Chowan County Court } June Term 1827

    Ordered, That Edward Garrett, Stephen Dolby, Samuel Simpson, Miles Skinner, Moses Burke and Willis Small, be appointed Patrollers in Captn. Paine's District; Edward Garrett to be Captain.
Test. Henry Wills, Clk

****

No 368
his
Jacob X Spivey
Mark
Test. Wm. Bratten

State of North Carolina }
Chowan County Court } November Term 1843

    Ordered, That Jacob Spivey be allowed the sum of Four Dollars for one years Services as a Patroll in the Upper District, under Thomas

Chowan County
Patrol Records

Bogue Captain and that the Sheriff pay the same when in funds and be allowed in in the settlement of his Accounts. $4
Issued 9th April 1844
Test. T.V. Hathaway, Clk

****

To Henderson D. Jones
For Service and return to June Term 1827
Executed by delivering a Copy of this Order to
Henderson D Jones, 31st March 1827
Wm D Rascoe, Shff

State of North Carolina   }
Chowan County Court   } March Term !827

    Ordered, That Obed Small, David Small and Thomas Simons, be appointed Patrollers in Green Hall District, under Henderson D. Jones, in lieu of three others deceased.
Test. Henry Wills, Clk

****

Robert R. Felton & others, Patrol order
To be returned to August term 1844
Executed by a Copy being left with
Robert R. Felton, July 4th 1844
W.D. Rascoe, Shff
By B Nixon, D Shff

State of North Carolina   }
Chowan County Court   } May Term 1844

    Ordered, that Robert R. Felton, Joseph J. Byrum, John W. Hudson, Thomas Boyce, and Henry Boyce be appointed a Patrol in the Rockahock District and that Robert R. Felton be Captain.
Issued 27th May 1844
Test. T.V. Hathaway, Clk

****

Chowan County
Patrol Records

James Norcom Junr., & others, Patrol Order
To be returned to November Term 1844
Executed by delivering a Copy of the within
To Jas: Norcom Junr., August 24th 1844
T.S. Hoskins, Shff

State of North Carolina }
Chowan County Court } August Term 1844

Ordered, that James Norcom Junr., Ephraim B. Davenport, Edwin M. Moore, William Norcom, William A. Littlejohn, Townsend Wright, and Hezekiah G. Arnold be appointed a Patrol in the District below Edenton and that James Norcom Junr., be Captain.
Issued 19th Augst. 1844
Test. T.V. Hathaway, Clk

****

Robert Creecy & als
Patroll on Capt Benburys District
June Term 1828
Rec'd a Copy of this order

State of North Carolina }
Chowan County Court } June Term 1828

Ordered that, Robert Creecy, Charles W Meseson[?], Lemuel B. Halsey, Allen Wood & Nathaniel Alexander, be appointed Patroll for Capt. Benburys District, and that Robert Creecy, be appointed Capt. Of said Patroll
Test. Edm. Hoskins, Clk

****

Edm Brinkley, Order
Capt. Paines Dist Patroll
Septr Term 1828
Executed by delivering a Copy of this Order
to Edm. Brinkley, 7th Oct 1828
Wm. D. Rascoe, Shff

Chowan County
Patrol Records

State of North Carolina }
Chowan County Court } September Term 1828

    Order that Edmund Brinkley, George Walton, Paul Bunch, Benjamin Bateman & Thomas Cockran, be appointed as Patroll in Capt. Paines District and that Edmond Brinkley be Capt. Of said Patroll.
Test. Edm Hoskins, Clk

****

Robert R. Felton, Capt. & others
Patroll Order
To be returned to November Term 1845

Executed by leaving a Copy of this Order at the dwelling House of R.R. Felton Esqr., Sept the 26th 1845
A Small, Dpt Shff
Thos T. Hoskins, Shff

State of North Carolina }
Chowan County Court } August Term 1845

Ordered, That Robert R. Felton, Joseph J. Byrum, John W. Hudson, Thomas Boyce and Charles Smith be appointed Patroll in the Rockahock District and that Robert R. Felton be Captain
Issued Augst 1845
Test. T.V. Hathaway, Clk

****

Geo F. Walton et als
Patroll in the upper District June Term 1829
Rec'd a Copy of this order from the Clk

State of North Carolina }
Chowan County } June Term 1829

Chowan County
Patrol Records

Ordered that George F. Walton, Jesse Welch, Wynns Baker, Wm Bush, Patrick Powell and Samuel Reddick be appointed Patroll in the upper District.
Test. Edm. Hoskins, Clk

****

Miles Goodwin Capt. & others
Patroll Order
To be returned to November Term 1845

Executed by leaving a Copy of the Within order with Myles Goodwin 11th Sept 1845
A Small, Dept Shff
Thos Hoskins, Shff

State of North Carolina }
Chowan County Court } August Term 1845

Ordered, that Miles Goodwin, Thomas Evans, Richard Goodwin, William Privitt Junr., Thomas Cochrain Junr., and Caleb Perry be appointed Patroll in the Middle District, and that Miles Goodwin be Captain
Issued Augt 1845
Test. T.V. Hathaway, Clk

****

Patroll Order for Middle District
To be left with Ephraim Goodwin Capt.
Patrollers Order

State of North Carolina }
Chowan County Court } August Term 1840

Ordered, that Ephraim Goodwin, Sandford E. Goodwin, Henry Hurdle, James Robertson Junr., and Thomas Cochrain Junr., be appointed Patroll in the Middle District, and that Ephraim Goodwin be Captain.
Issued 14th August 1840
Test John Bush, Clk

Chowan County
Patrol Records

By T.V. Hathaway, D Clk

****

Patroll Order for Noah Ward & others
To be left with Noah Ward, Captain
Let the within named persons be
Allowed five Dollars each

State of North Carolina   } May Term 1840
Chowan County Court   }

   Ordered, That Noah Ward, Lemuel Hurdle, Elisha Bunch, Thomas Bouge and Jacob Spivey be appointed Patroll in the Upper District, and that Noah Ward be Captain.
Issued 22nd May 1840
Test. John Bush, Clk
By T.V. Hathaway, D. Clk

****

Miles Goodwin & others, Patroll Order
To be left with Miles Goodwin, Capt.
Order to be paid

State of North Carolina   }
Chowan County Court   } August Term 1845

   Ordered that Miles Goodwin, Wm Roberts, Thomas Evans, Richard Goodwin, William Privitt Junr., Thomas Cochrain Junr., and Caleb Perry, be appointed Patroll in the Middle District and that Miles Goodwin be Captain.
Issued Augst 1845
Test. T.V. Hathaway, Clk

****

Patrol Order, Ephraim Goodwin, Capt., & others
To be returned to November Term 1841

Chowan County
Patrol Records

Executed by delivering a Copy of this Order with Ephraim Goodwin, 16th Aug. 1841
W.D. Rascoe, Shff

State of North Carolina }
Chowan County Court } August Term 1841

Ordered, That Ephraim Goodwin, Henry Goodwin, Henry Hurdle, James Robertson Junr., Thomas Cochrain Junr., and William Privitt Junr., be appointed a Patroll in the Middle District, and that Ephraim Goodwin be Captain.
Issued 16th August 1841
Test. John Bush, Clk
By T.V. Hathaway, D. Clk

****

John Bond & others, Patrol Order
To be left with John Bond, Captain

Ordered that the Within Named be allowed the Lawful fee and that Abram Bonner be appointed in place of E. Evans
Thos J Charlton

State of North Carolina }
Chowan County Court } November Term 1844

Ordered, that John Bond, Samuel Eshon, Elijah Smith and Edwin Evans, be appointed a Patrol in the Green Hall District and that John Bond be Captain.
Issued 15th Nov 1844
Test. T.V. Hathaway, Clk

****

Miles Goodwin & others, Patrol Order
To be left with Miles Goodwin, Capt.

State of North Carolina }
Chowan County Court } August Term 1844

Chowan County
Patrol Records

Ordered, that Miles Goodwin, Thomas Evans, Joseph B. Newby, Richard Goodwin, William Privitt Junr., and Thomas Cochrain Junr., be appointed a Patrol in the Middle District and that Miles Goodwin be Captain
Issued 19th Augst 1844.
Test T.V. Hathaway, Clk

****

Patrol Order, Chas. G. Haughton, Capt. & others
To be returned to November Term 1841

Executed by delivering a Copy of this Order to Charles G. Haughton 16th Aug. 1841.
W.D. Rascoe, Shff

State of North Carolina   }
Chowan County Court   } August Term 1841

Ordered, That Charles G. Haughton, John W. Roberts, Frederick L. Roberts, Frederick C. Gregory, Thomas Hoskins and William A. Littlejohn, be appointed a Patrol in the District below Edenton, and that Charles G. Haughton be Captain.
Issued 16th August 1841
Test. John Bush, Clk
By T.V. Hathaway, D. Clk

****

Patrol Order, Ephraim Goodwin Capt. & others

Ordered that the same person be appointed Patrol, August Term 1842. To be left with Ephraim Goodwin, Capt.

Ordered that the Members of this Patrol receive Ten Dollars each
Robertson Issued
Goodwin Issued

State of North Carolina   }

Chowan County
Patrol Records

Chowan County Court   } August Term 1841

Ordered, That Ephraim Goodwin, Henry Hurdle, James Robertson Junr., Thomas Cochrain Junr., and William Privitt Junr., be appointed a Patroll in the Middle District, and that Ephraim Goodwin be Captain.
Issued 16th August 1841
Test. John Bush, Clk
By T.V. Hathaway, D. Clk

****

Chas. E. Johnson & others, Order Patrol Committee
To be returned to Nov. Term 1846

Executed by delivering a Copy of the within to Chas. E. Johnson, Sept. 3rd 1846
T.S. Hoskins, Shff

State of North Carolina   }
Chowan County Court   } August Term 1846

Ordered, that Charles E. Johnson, Thomas Satterfield and Robert R. Felton be appointed a Committee to appoint such a Patroll in the Rockyhock District as may be necessary for its Protection.
Issued Augt. 26, 1846
Test. T.V. Hathaway, Clk

****

Patrol Order, Robert R. Felton, Capt. & others
To be left with Robt. R. Felton, Capt.

Ordered that the Members of this Patrol Receive Six Dollars each.

State of North Carolina   }
Chowan County Court   } August Term 1841

Ordered, That Robert Felton, Charles Smith, Nathaniel Bond Junr., John Hudson and William Smith Junr., be appointed a Patroll in the Rockahock District, and that Robert R. Felton be Captain.

Chowan County
Patrol Records

Issued 16th August 1841
Test. John Bush, Clk
By T.V. Hathaway, D. Clk

****

Joshua Skinner & others, Order
Patrol Committee
To be returned to Nov Term 1846

Executed by delivering a Copy of the within to Joshua Skinner Sept 3rd 1846
T.S. Hoskins, Shff

State of North Carolina }
Chowan County Court } August Term 1846

Ordered, that Joshua Skinner, William Benbury, and Joseph Norcom, be appointed a Committee to appoint such a Patroll in the District below Edenton as may be necessary for its Protection
Issued Augst. 26th 1846
Test. T.V. Hathaway, Clk

****

Patrol Order
James Norcom Junr., Capt., & others
To be returned to November Term 1841

Executed by delivering a Copy of this Order to James Norcom Junr., 23rd 1841
W.D. Rascoe, Shff

State of North Carolina }
Chowan County Court } August Term 1841

Ordered, that James Norcom Junr., Edwin M. Moore, William Norcom, John Lemuel Leary, and Joshua Skinner, be appointed a Patrol in the District below Edenton, and that James Norcom Junr., be Captain.
Issued 16th August 1841

Chowan County
Patrol Records

Test. John Bush, Clk
By T.V. Hathaway, D. Clk

****

Baker F. Welch & others, Order
Patrol Committee
To be Returned to Nov. Term 1846

Executed by delivering a copy of the within to Baker F. Welch, Sept. 3rd 1846
T.S. Hoskins, Shff

State of North Carolina }
Chowan County Court } August Term 1846

    Ordered, that Baker F. Welch, Jacob Cullen and William Hurdle be appointed a Committee to appoint such a Patroll as may be necessary in the Upper District for its Protection.
Issued August 26th 1846
Test. T.V. Hathaway, Clk

****

Hen'd Simpson & others, Order
Patroll Committee
To be returned to Nov. Term 1846

Executed by delivering a Copy of the within to Henderson Simpson, Sept. 3rd 1846
T.S. Hoskins, Shff

State of North Carolina }
Chowan County Court } August Term 1846

    Ordered, that Henderson Simpson, William Bratten and Daniel V. Etheridge be appointed a Committee to appoint such Patroll in the Middle District, as may be necessary for its Protection.
Issued August 26th 1846
Test. T.V. Hathaway, Clk

Chowan County
Patrol Records

****

No. 256
Rec'd payment from WD rascoe, Shff
Thomas Cochrain Junr.

State of North Carolina }
Chowan County Court } August Term 1842

    Ordered, That Thomas Cochrain Junr., be allowed Six dollars for one years service as Patroll in the Middle District under Ephraim Goodwin Capt. And that the Sheriff pay the same when in funds and be allowed it in settlement of his accounts. $6
Test. T.V. Hathaway, Clk

****

Patrol Order, Wm Norcom & others
To be returned to Feby Term 1847
Executed by delivering a Copy Decr. 21st 1846
T.S. Hoskins, Shff

State of North Carolina }
Chowan County Court } November Term 1846

    Ordered, that William Norcom, William D. Lowther Junr., Nathaniel J. Beasley and Joseph J. Jordan be appointed a Patroll in the District below Edenton, and that Wm. Norcom be Captain.
Test. T.V. Hathaway, Clk

****

No. 262
Rec'd payment from WD Rascoe, Shff
Wm L. Smith

State of North Carolina }
Chowan County Court } August Term 1842

Chowan County
Patrol Records

Ordered, that William Smith Junr., be allowed Six dollars for one years services as Patroll in the District of Rockahock under Robert R. Felton Captain, and that the Sheriff pay the same when in funds and be allowed it in settlement of his Accounts. $6
Test. T.V. Hathaway, Clk

****

Patroll Order, Richd Paxton & others
To be returned to Feby Term 1847
Executed by delivering a Copy Decr. 22nd 1846
T.S. Hoskins, Shff

State of North Carolina }
Chowan County Court   } November Term 1846

Ordered, that Richard Paxton, Ephraim Davenport, Joseph Moore and Asa Ainsley be appointed a patroll in the District below Edenton and that Richard Paxton be Captain.
Test. T.V. Hathaway, Clk

****

No. 261
Rec'd payment from WD Rascoe, Shff

State of North Carolina }
Chowan County Court   } August Term 1842

Ordered, that Robert R. Felton, Captain, be allowed Six dollars for one years services as Patroll in the District of Rockahock, and that the Sheriff pay the same when in funds and be allowed it in settlement of his Accounts. $6
Test. T.V. Hathaway, Clk

****

Patrol Order
Wm. A. Littlejohn & others
To be returned to Feby Term 1847

Chowan County
Patrol Records

Executed by delivering a Copy Decr 18th 1846
T.S. Hoskins, Shff

State of North Carolina }
Chowan County Court   } November Term 1846

    Ordered, that William A. Littlejohn, Frederick C. Gregory, David Furlough and John Parker be appointed a patroll in the District below Edenton and that Wm. A. Littlejohn be Captain
Test. T.V. Hathaway, Clk

****

No. 253
Rec'd payment from WD Rascoe, Shff
His
James X Robertson
Mark
Witness, Geo. M. Williams

State of North Carolina }
Chowan County Court   } August Term 1842

    Ordered, that James Robertson be allowed Six dollars for serving as a Patroll in the Middle District for twelve months, under Ephraim Goodwin Captain and that the Sheriff pay the same when in funds and be allowed it in settlement of his Accounts. $6
Test. T.V. Hathaway, Clk

****

Saml Eshon & others, Order
Patrol Committee
To be returned to Nov. Term 1846

Executed by delivering a Copy of the within to Samuel Eshon, Sept. 3rd 1846
T.S. Hoskins, Shff

State of North Carolina }

Chowan County
Patrol Records

Chowan County Court   } August Term 1846

    Ordered, that Samuel Eshon, Peter F. White & John Bonner, be appointed a Committee to appoint such a Patrol in the Green Hall District, as may be necessary for its Protection
Issued Augst 26th 1846
Teste. T.V. Hathaway, Clk

****

No. 255
Rec'd Payment from W.D. Rascoe, Shff
Charles Smith

State of North Carolina   }
Chowan County Court   } August Term 1842

    Ordered, that Charles Smith be allowed Six dollars for one years service as Patroll in the District of Rockahock under Robert R. Felton Capt. And that the Sheriff pay the same when in funds and be allowed it in settlement of his Accounts. $6
Test. T.V. Hathaway, Clk

****

Wm J. Holley, Saml Simpson & Martin B. Simpson
Order, Patroll Committee Middle District
To be returned to November Term 1848
Executed by Delivering a Copy to the parties concerned
T.S. Hoskins, Shff

State of North Carolina   }
Chowan County Court   } August Term 1848

    Ordered, that William J. Holley, Samuel Simpson and Martin B. Simpson be appointed Patrol Committee in the Middle District, in place of the former Committee, resigned.
Issued August 21st 1848
Test. T.V. Hathaway, Clk

Chowan County
Patrol Records

****

No. 278

State of North Carolina }
Chowan County Court } November Term 1842

     Ordered, that David Dickinson be allowed Four dollars and seventy five cents the Amount of his Account for work done on the Public Buildings and that the Sheriff pay the same when in funds and be allowed it in settlement of his Accounts. $4. 75/100
Test. T.V. Hathaway, Clk

****

Gideon Byrum's Receipt for Patrol order, $6
Paid by T.S. Hoskins, Shff & &C - July 31st 1848

Received of Tho S. Hoskins Sheriff of Six Dollars in [?] Patrol Order this 31st July 1848
Gideon Byrum

****

No. 273

Pay the within to Joseph J. Byrum the Amt. Of the within he having served in my place as Patrol

His   His
Nathl X Bond Junr.   Joseph X Byrum
Mark   Mark

Test. T.V. Hathaway
Saml T. Bond

State of North Carolina }
Chowan County Court } August Term 1842

     Ordered, that Nathaniel Bond Junr., be allowed Six dollars for his Services as a Patroll in the Rockahock District for one year, under Robert

Chowan County
Patrol Records

R. Felton Captain and that the Sheriff pay the same when in finds and be allowed it in settlement of his Accounts. $6
Test. T.V. Hathaway, Clk

****

Richd. Goodwin's Receipt $6 As Patrol, Pd.
Aug 7th 1848
By T.S. H. Shff

Rec'd Aug 7th 1848 from T.S. Hoskins, Shff, Six dollars & 20 cts, in part of allowance made by Court for Patrol services.
Richard Goodwin

****

Pursuant to the order of the County Court of Chowan made at August Term 1846, The Committee of Patrols for Rockahock Composed of Charles E Johnson, R.R. Felton and Thos Satterfield -- this day 1st February 1848 at the House of Charles E Johnson and appointed the following Persons to Act as a Patrol Company for the District of Rockahock (viz) From the 5th Septr. 1847

Bartimus Nixon Captain of the Company

Joseph J Byrum }
Thos Boyce   } 10 apiece
Gideon Byrum   }

Thos Satterfield
Chas. E. Johnson
R.R. Felton

Bartimus Nixon, Captain Sworn before this time of the Court as to the performance of the men acting under him, as [?] there as patrol.

Feby Term 1849 - Co. of Pleas & qr. Sessions for Chowan County.

****

Patrol Order for Middle District
To be returned to Nov. Term 1850

For Miles Goodwin, Capt., Thos. Cochran Junr., Wm Creecy, John W. Hudson & Wm N. Bunch

Chowan County
Patrol Records

Executed by leaving a Copy of the within with Miles Goodwin et als, Oct. 1850
T.S. Hoskins, Shff

North Carolina }
Chowan County Court } August Term 1850

    Ordered that the following persons be appointed a patrol for the Middle District Viz Myles Goodwin Capt., Thomas Cochraine Junr., William Creecy, John W. Hudson & William N Bunch
Wm R Skinner, Clk

****

Patrol Order

William Norcom, Jos: Moore & S.A.W. Righton.
Aug: Term 1850, to be returned

Executed by notifying all the parties, & giving a Copy to Eph. Davenport, May 1850
T.S. Hoskins, Shff

North Carolina }
Chowan County Court } May Term 1850

    Ordered that Ephraim Davenport, Joseph Moore, William Norcom & Stark A. W. Righton be appointed a patrol for the District below Edenton.
Issued 14th May 1850
Test. Wm R. Skinner, Clk

****

Patrol Order for John Bond et als
To Aug. Term 1850

To be Returned, To Wit: John Bond, Wm. E. Bond, George Bond & Ephm. B. Elliott

Chowan County
Patrol Records

Executed by notifying the parties, & giving a Copy to John Bond - 1850
T.S. Hoskins, Shff

North Carolina   }
Chowan County Court   } May Term 1850

   Ordered that John Bond, William E. Bond, George Bond & Ephraim B. Elliott be appointed a patrol for the Green Hall District.
Issued 14th May 1850
Test. Wm R. Skinner, Clk

****

Patrol Order For Kedar Winslow
To be returned to Feb. term 1851
Executed by serving a Copy of the within
Nov. 15th 1850
T.S. Hoskins, Shff

State of North Carolina   }
Chowan County Court   } Nov Term 1850

   Ordered that Kedar Winslow, Righton Ward, Andrew Ward & Allen Ward be appointed a patrol for the Upper District and that Kedar Winslow be Captain of said Patrol
Issued the 13th Nov. 1850
Wm. Skinner, Clk

****

Patrol Order, Sound Side below Edenton
Stark A Righton, Capt
To be returned to Nov. Term 1851

Executed by delivering a Copy of the within to Stark A. Righton, Capt, et als, August 21st 1851
T.S. Hoskins, Shff

State of North Carolina   }
Chowan County Court   } August Term 1851

Chowan County
Patrol Records

Ordered that the following persons be appointed a patrol on the Sound Side below Edenton Viz Stark A. Righton, Capt., Joshua Skinner, Edward S Riggs, Wm. J. Leary & Elbridge Leary
Issued 12th Aug 1851
Wm. Skinner, Clk

****

Patrol Order, Green Hall For John Bond et als
To be returned to Nov. Term 1851

Executed by delivering a Copy of the within to John Bond &c, Sept. 4th 1851.
T.S. Hoskins, Shff

State of North Carolina }
Chowan County Court } Aug. Term 1851

Ordered, that the following persons be appointed a patrol for the Green Hall District, Viz John Bond, Capt., Edwin Evans, William Fleetwood, George Bond, Martin Harrell & Abner Dail.
Issued 12th Aug 1851
Wm R Skinner, Clk

****

Patrol Order, Below Edenton For John Bonner et als
To Nov. term 1851

Executed by delivering a Copy of the within to John Bonner, &c. Aug. 20th 1851
T.S. Hoskins, Clk

State of North Carolina }
Chowan County Court } August Term 1851

Ordered that the following persons be appointed a patrol below Edenton viz John Bonner, Capt., William H. Standin, Benjamin Thatch, John Parker & John Moore

Chowan County
Patrol Records

Issued 12th Aug 1851
Wm. R. Skinner, Clk

****

Jackson H. Moore's Receipt
Patrol, $4. Pd. Aug. 7th 1852
By T.S. Hoskins, Shff

Rec'd Aug: 7th 1852 from T.S. Hoskins, Shff four Dollars, being the Amt. Allowed me by Court, as one of the Patrol in the Upper District, the past year. J. H. Moore, $4

****

Cader Winslow &c, $8. Paid by T.S. Hoskins, Shff. Aug: 1852

Paid Jackson Moore $4, and Cader Winslow four Dollars, for their services as Patrollers, as ordered by the Court, - making eight dollars. Aug. 8th 1852. By T.S. Hoskins, Shff

****

Patrol Order for the Upper District
To be returned to Feb. Term 1852
For Jas Cannon et als

Executed by leaving a Copy of the within with Jas: J. Cannon et als - November 21st 1851
T.S. Hoskins, Shff

State of North Carolina }
Chowan County Court } Nov Term 1851

  Ordered that James J. Cannon, Dossey Welch, Noah Ward & Drew Welch, be and they are hereby appointed a patrol for the Upper District and that said Cannon act as Captain of said Patrol
Issued the 13th Nov 1851
Wm. R. Skinner, Clk

Chowan County
Patrol Records

****

Patrol Order for Rockyhock District
To be returned to Feb. term 1852

Executed by leaving a Copy of the within, with Jos: J. Bynum et als, Nov. 21st 1851. T.S. Hoskins, Shff

State of North Carolina   }
Chowan County Court   } Nov. term 1851

Ordered that Joseph J. Byrum, Miles Ashley, Charles Smith & William Trivett Junr., be appointed a patrol for Rockyhock District and that William Privett act as Captain of said patrol.
Issued 13th Nov 1857
Wm. R. Skinner, Clk

****

Patrol Order For Martin B. Simpson et als
Nov. Term 1852

Executed by leaving a Copy of the within with Martin B. Simpson, Aug. 25th 1852. T.S. Hoskins, Shff

State of North Carolina   }
Chowan County Court   } August Term 1852

Ordered that Martin B Simpson, Josiah Coffield, Jeremiah Evans, Myles Goodwin and William N Bunch be and they are appointed a patrol for the Middle District and that said Martin B. Simpson act as Captain.
Issued the 12th day of August 1852.
Wm R. Skinner, Clk

****

Middle District, Patrol Order
To be returned to Feb. Term 1852

Chowan County
Patrol Records

Executed by leaving a Copy of the within with John Coffield et als, Nov. 21st 1851. T.S. Hoskins, Shff

State of North Carolina   }
Chowan County Court   } Nov Term 1851

      Ordered that John Coffield, Josiah Coffield, Martin B. Simpson & Williamson Goodwin be and they are hereby appointed a patrol for the Middle District and that said Simpson act as Captain of said patrol.
Issued 13th Nov. 1851
Wm R. Skinner, Clk

****

Patrol Order For Wm. Bonner et als
Aug. Term 1852

Executed by summoning the parties & leaving a Copy of the within order, with Wm. Bonner, June 1852
T.S. Hoskins, Shff

State of North Carolina   }
Chowan County Court   } May Term 1852

      Ordered that Trotman H. Ward, Peyton Bass, Wm. Bonner, Joseph Copeland & George Bond be and they are hereby appointed a patrol for Cowpen Neck District and that said William Bonner act as Captain of said patrol.
Issued the 4th May 1852
Wm. R Skinner, Shff

****

Patrol Order For M.B. Simpson et als
To be returned to May Term 1852
Executed by delivering a copy
T.S. Hoskins, Shff

State of North Carolina   }
Chowan County Court   } February Term 1852

Chowan County
Patrol Records

Ordered that Josiah Coffield, Martin B. Simpson, Thomas White, James L. Roberts and Jeremiah Evans be and they are hereby appointed a patrol for the Middle District and that Martin B Simpson act as Captain of said patrol.
Issued the 11th Feb 1852
Wm. R. Skinner, Clk

****

Patrol Order To be left with Martin B. Simpson
From Feb. Term 1852
From T.S. Hoskins, Shff

State of North Carolina }
Chowan County Court } Feb Term 1852

Ordered that Josiah Coffield, Martin B Simpson, Thomas White, James L. Roberts and Jeremiah Evans be and they are hereby appointed a patrol for the Middle Districts and that Martin B. Simpson act as Captain of said Patrol.
Issued the 11th day of February 1852
Wm. R. Skinner, Clk

In the place of James Roberts, put Myles Goodwin - In the place of Thos White, put Nuby Bunch, August Term 1852. Al[?] Chishire For chairman.

****

Patrol Order, a Copy to be left with Trotman H. Ward

Executed by summoning the parties, & leaving a Copy of the within with Trotman H. Ward, Jan 1853
T.S. Hoskins, Shff
From May term 1853.
Shff's fees $2.10

State of North Carolina }
Chowan County Court } May Term 1853

Chowan County
Patrol Records

Ordered that Trotman H Ward, Isaac Kail, William H. Todd, James Wilson, Seth B Parker, Isaac Smith, & Daniel Ward, be and they are hereby appointed a patrol for Green Hall District, and that said Trotman H Ward act as Captain.
Issued the 9th day of May 1853
Wm R Skinner, Clk

****

Order Appointing Patrol Committee
Viz: John H. Leary, C. w. Mixon & W.D. Lowther
For below Edenton, from Novr. Term 1853
To February term 1854

Executed by notifying the persons herein named, & leaving a Copy with John H. Leary Esq. Nov. 30th 1853
T.S. Hoskins, Shff, Shff's fees 90 cts

State of North Carolina   }
Chowan County Court   } Nov Term 1853

Ordered that John H Leary, Charles W. Mixson & William D. Lowther be and they are hereby appointed patrol Committee for the District below Edenton.
Issued the 18th day of Nov 1853
Wm. R. Skinner, Clk

****

Order appointing Patrol Committee
Viz: Thos. D. Warren, T.L. Skinner & Jordan D. Elliott
For District of Edenton and Green Hall
From Novr. Term 1853
To February Term 1854

Executed by notifying the persons herein named, & leaving a Copy with Thos. D. Warren Esq Nov. 30th 1853
T.S. Hoskins, Shff, Shff's fees 90 cts.

State of North Carolina   }

Chowan County
Patrol Records

Chowan County Court   } November Term 1853

Ordered that Thomas D Warren, T. L. Skinner, and Jordan D Elliott be and they are hereby appointed Patrol Committee for the District of Edenton and Green Hall.
Issued the 18th day of Nov. 1853
Wm R. Skinner, Clk

****

Patrol Order, Rockyhock District
Feb. Term 1853

Charles Smith, Capt., William Privitt Junr., Joseph J. Bynum, Myles Ashley & William Perry

Executed by delivering a copy to the parties, Decr. 1852
T.S. Hoskins, Shff, Shff's fees $1.50

State of North Carolina   }
Chowan County Court   } November Term 1852

Ordered that Charles Smith, William Privett Jr., Joseph J. Byrum, Myles Ashley & William Perry be and they are hereby appointed a patrol for the Rockyhock District and that said Charles Smith act as Captain of said patrol.
Issued 12th Nov 1852
Wm R. Skinner, Clk

****

Patrol Order, Below Edenton, Feb. Term 1852

John E. Leary, Captn., Joseph Moran, Isaac Moran, Stark A. Righton, & Robert Johnson.

Executed by summoning the Parties, & leaving a Copy with John E. Leary, Captn., Decr. 10th 1852
T.S. Hoskins, Shff
Shff's fees $1.50

Chowan County
Patrol Records

State of North Carolina }
Chowan County Court } Nov Term 1852

Ordered that John E. Leary, Joseph Moran, Isaac Moran, Stark A. Righton & Robert Johnson be and they are hereby appointed a Patrol below Edenton, and that said John E. Leary act as Captain of said patrol.
Issued 12th Nov 1852
Wm. R. Skinner, Clk

****

Patrol Order For Middle District
Nov Term 1853

Executed, by delivering a Copy of the within, to Myles Goodwin, Capt., September 1853.
T.S. Hoskins, Shff

State of North Carolina }
Chowan County Court } August Term 1853

Ordered that Myles Goodwin, John Pierce, John Goodwin, Allen H Perry & Williamson Goodwin be and they are hereby appointed a Patrol for the Middle District, and that said Myles Goodwin act as Captain thereof
Issued the 9th August 1853
Wm. R. Skinner, Clk

****

Patrol Order for Green Hall District
To Aug: Term 1853

Executed by leaving a Copy of the within, with the parties
T.S. Hoskins, Shff

State of North Carolina }
Chowan County, Court } May Term 1853

Chowan County
Patrol Records

Ordered that Trotman H Ward, Isaac Kail, William H. Todd, James Wilson, Seth B. Parker, Isaac Smith, & Daniel Ward be and they are hereby appointed a patrol for Green Hall District and that said Trotman H Ward act as Captain.
Issued the 9th day of May 1853
Wm R. Skinner, Clk

****

Order Appointing Patrol Committee
Viz: H. Simpson, Saml. Simpson & Martin B. Simpson
For Middle District from Novr. Term 1853
To February Term 1854

Executed by notifying the persons herein Named, & leaving a Copy with H. Simpson Esq. Nov. 23rd 1853.
T.S. Hoskins, Shff, Shff's fees, 70 cts

State of North Carolina }
Chowan County Court } Nov Term 1853

Ordered that Henderson Simpson, Samuel Simpson and Martin B. Simpson be and they are hereby appointed Patrol Committee for the Middle District
Issued the 18th day Nov 1853
Wm. Skinner, Clk

****

Order appointing Patrol Committee
Viz: R.R. Felton, B. Nixon & Fred. Bunch
For Rockahock District
From Novr. Term 1853
To February Term 1854

Executed by notifying the persons herein named, & leaving a Copy with R. R. Felton Esq. Nov. 30th 1853.
T.S. Hoskins, Shff, Shff's fees 70 cts

State of North Carolina }

Chowan County
Patrol Records

Chowan County Court } November Term 1853

Ordered that Robert R. Felton, Bartemius Nixon and Frederick Bunch be and they are hereby appointed Patrol Committee for the Rockyhock District.
Issued the 18th day of Nov. 1853
Wm R. Skinner, Clk

****

Order appointing Patrol Committee
Viz: B.F. Welch, W. H. Elliott & J. J. Cannon
For Upper District
From Novr. Term 1853
To February Term 1854

Executed by notifying the persons herein named, & leaving a Copy with B.F. Welch Esq. - Nov. 23rd 1853
T.S. Hoskins, Shff, Shff's fees 90 cts

State of North Carolina }
Chowan County Court } Nov Term 1853

Ordered that Baker F. Welch, William H. Elliott & James J. Cannon be and thaey are hereby appointed Patrol Committee for Upper District.
Issued the 18th day of Nov 1853
Wm R Skinner, Clk

****

Ordered by the Court that Cullen Halsey, John Perry, William Perry & John Saterfield be allowed eight Dollars for service as patrol
J D [?]

We the Patrol Committee, met and appointed the following Men as Patrols, for the district of Rockyhock for the Ensuing Year Viz: Collen Halsy, Capt., John Perry, Wm. Perry & John Satterfield, (Subordinates) Decr. 31st 1853
R R Felton, B. Hin[?], Fred Bunch

Chowan County
Patrol Records

****

William Privitt Junr., Capt. Of Patrol Company for the Middle District

Ordered by the Court that William Privitt, William M Bunch, Jeremiah Evans and John Pierce. Be allowed twenty Dollars for the within order.

State of North Carolina }
Chowan County Court }

We the undersigned Patrol Committee, being appointed by the Court at November Term 1853 for the Middle District have proceeded to appoint the following named persons a Patrol for the Middle District - William Privitt, Junr., Capt., Richard Small, Thomas Evins, William N Bunch, Jeremiah Evins, John Pierce, H Simpson, Saml Simpson & Martin B. Simpson
This December 8th 1853

****

Patrol Order for T.H. Ward et als for Nov term 1854
Executed by a Copy left with TH Ward, P F White, Shff

State of North Carolina }
Chowan County Court } August Term 1854

Ordered that Trotman H Ward, Isaac Kail, James Wilson, Seth B Parker, Isaac Smith, Daniel Ward and John Bass be and they are hereby appointed a patrol for Green Hall District and that said Trotman H Ward act as Captain thereof
Issued the 21st August 1854
Wm R Skinner, Clk

****

Patrol Order Below Edenton
May Term 1854, Chowan County Court
Joshua C. Skinner Esq. And others

Chowan County
Patrol Records

Executed by leaving a Copy of the within, with Joshua C. Skinner
T.S. Hoskins, Shff

State of North Carolina }
Chowan County Court } February Term 1854

    Ordered that Joshua C. Skinner, John Skinner, Joseph Moran, John Bonner and Dr. W J Leary be and they are hereby appointed a Patrol below Edenton as Company No. 1 and that said Joshua C. Skinner act as Captain thereof
Wm R. Skinner, Clk

****

    Order appointing Patrol Committee For Green Hall
    Aug Term 1855

Executed by a Copy left with Samuel Eshon
P F White, Shff

State of North Carolina }
Chowan County Court } May Term 1855

    Ordered that Samuel Eshon, James Bonner and Edwin Evans be and they are hereby appointed a patrol Committee in Green Hall District for one Year.
Wm R Skinner, Clk

****

    Order appointing Patrol Committee
    For Rockyhock District 1855, August Term

Executed by a Copy of the within left with West Leary 5th June 1855
P. F. White, Shff

State of North Carolina }
Chowan County Court } May Term 1855

Chowan County
Patrol Records

Ordered that Robert R. Felton, John B. Webb and West Leary be and they are hereby appointed a patrol Committee in Rockyhock District for one Year.
Wm. R. Skinner, Clk

****

Order appointing Patrol Committee Below Edenton, 1855
Aug. Term 1855

Executed by a Copy left with Edw. Wood
P. F. White, Shff

State of North Carolina }
Chowan County Court } May Term 1855

Ordered that Charles W. Mixson, Edward Wood and William D Lowther be and they are hereby appointed a Patrol Committee in the District below Edenton for one year.
Wm R Skinner, Clk

****

Patrol Order For the Middle District
February Term 1857

Executed by a Copy left at the residence of John R. Simpson Nov. 18th 1856
P F White, Shff

State of North Carolina }
Chowan County Court } November Term 1836

Ordered that John R. Simpson, Thomas J. Leary, Allen H. Perry, Myles C. Brinkley and Richard Small be and they are hereby appointed a Patrol for the Middle District and that said John R. Simpson act as Captain thereof
Wm. R. Skinner, Clk

****

Chowan County
Patrol Records

Patrol Order For Edenton
Feby Term 1857

Executed by a Copy left with Jas. Warren, Nov. 18th 1856
P.F. White, Shff

State of North Carolina }
Chowan County Court } Nov Term 1856

    Ordered that James Norcom, Joseph Moran, Stark A. Righton, Charles Woodley and Joseph Z. [?]att be and they are hereby appointed a Patrol for the Town of Edenton and that said James Norcom act as Captain thereof.
Wm R. Skinner, Clk

****

Patrol Order For Lower District
Wm D. Lowther, John Smith, Jos Moran, R.S. Pratt & Wm. Waff
Nov Term 1856

Executed by a Copy left with William D. Louther
PF White, Shff

State of North Carolina }
Chowan County Court } Aug Term 1856

    Ordered that William D. Lowther, John Smith, Joseph Moran, Robert S. Pratt and William Waff be and they are hereby appointed a patrol for the Lower District and that William D Lowther act as Captain thereof.
Wm. R. Skinner, Clk

****

Patrol Order For Jeremiah Evans & others
Feby Term 1856
Executed, PF White, Shff

State of North Carolina }

Chowan County
Patrol Records

Chowan County Court   } Nov Term 1855

    Ordered that Jeremiah Evans, William N. Bunch, William Privitt Junr., Williamson Goodwin and John Goodwin be and they are hereby appointed a patrol for the Middle District and that said Jeremiah Evans act as Captain thereof.
Wm R Skinner, Clk

****

Patrol Order For A. J. Glover et als
March Term 1857

Executed by a Copy left with A.J. Glover Decr. 22nd 1857
P.F. White, Shff

State of North Carolina   }
Chowan County Court   } Decr. Term 1857

    Ordered that A.J. Glover, Jas. N. Floyd, Joseph Moran, Robert S. Pratt, John Newman and John Bond be and they are hereby appointed a Patrol and that the be authorized to patrol below Edenton, in the Town of Edenton and in Green Hall District and that said Glover act as Captain thereof.
Wm. R. Skinner, Clk

****

Patrol Order Below Edenton For John Smith et als
March Term 1858

Executed by a Copy left with John Smith, Capt., Jany 2nd 1858
P F White, Shff

State of North Carolina   }
Chowan County Court   } Dec. Term 1857

    Ordered that John Smith, Moses Hobbs, Henry Halsey, Augustus Creecy, William Waff, John Bruner[?], and William Hedrick be and they

Chowan County
Patrol Records

are hereby appointed a Patrol below Edenton and that said John Smith act as Captain thereof.
Wm R Skinner, Clk

****

Patrol Order, Edenton District
Jas. Norcom Capt.
Dec. Term 1857

Executed by leaving a Copy with Jas Norcom Capt., Oct 10th 1857
P.F. White, Shff

State of North Carolina }
Chowan County Court } September Term 1857

    Ordered that James Norcom, R. T. Paine, Jos. G. Godfrey, Joseph Z. Pratt & Stark A. Righton be and they are hereby appointed a Patrol for Edenton District and that said James Norcom act as Captain thereof. Issued the 9th October 1857.
Wm. R. Skinner, Clk

****

Patrol Order For Green Hall
Febry. Term 1857

Executed by a Copy left with A.G. Glover, Nov 13th 1856
P.F. White, Shff

State of North Carolina }
Chowan County Court } November Term 1856

    Ordered that A.J. Glover, Mathew Rogers, John Bond, George Bond and Elijah Smith be and they are hereby appointed a Patrol for the Green Hall District and that said A.J. Glover act as Captain thereof.
Issued the 10th day of Nov 1856
Wm. R Skinner, Clk

****

Chowan County
Patrol Records

Patrol Order For Chas. S. Moore et als
Rockyhock, May Term 1857

Executed by a Copy left Feby 28th 1857
P.F. White, Shff

State of North Carolina   }
Chowan County Court   } February Term 1857

    Ordered that Charles S. Moore, John B. Satterfield, West Leary Junr., & Exum Goodwin be and they are hereby appointed a Patrol for Rockyhock District and that said Chas. S. Moore act as Captain thereof.
Issued 12th Feby. 1857
Wm R Skinner, Clk

****

Patrol Order For John Bonner, Capt.

William Smith, Jos Moran, John S. Leary, Moses Hobbs & Charles Woodley
Feby Term 1856

Executed by leaving a True Copy of the within with John Bonner
PF White, Shff

State of North Carolina   }
Chowan County Court   } Nov Term 1855

    Ordered that John Bonner, William Smith, Joseph Moran, John Leary, Moses Hobbs and Charles Woodley be and they are hereby appointed a Patrol below Edenton, and that said John Bonner act as Captain of said Patrol
Wm. R. Skinner, Clk

****

Patrol Order For the Upper District
February Term 1857

Chowan County
Patrol Records

Executed by a Copy left with Dossey Welch, Capt.
P F White, Shff

State of North Carolina }
Chowan County Court } Nov Term 1856

  Ordered that Dossey Welch, Thomas Copeland Junr., **[Faded]** Ward, William H. Winslow and Jackson H. Moore be and are hereby appointed a Patrol for the Upper District and that said Dossey Welch act as Captain thereof.
Issued the 10th day of Nov 1856
Wm R Skinner, Clk

****

Patrol, Charles Moore Esqr.
At Home

R.R. Felton and Frederick Bunch, having been appointed at June Term 1858 a Patrol Committee, they met and unanimously appointed Charles Moore Captain of the Patrol, and West R. Leary, John B. Satterfield, & Exum Goodwin Subordinates. They will please accept and discharge their duty, as Patroles for the District of Rockahock.
R.R. Felton, for the Commty

****

Patrol Committee Order For R. R. Felton, Fred Bunch
Sept Term 1858

Executed by leaving a Copy with RR Felton, Aug 14th 1858
P.F. White, Shff

State of North Carolina }
Chowan County Court } June Term 1858

  Ordered that Robert R. Felton and Frederick Bunch be and they are hereby appointed a Patrol Committee in Rockyhock District
Wm R. Skinner, Clk

Chowan County
Patrol Records

****

Patrol Commtee Order For Jas J. Cannon, W. H. Elliott

Executed by a Copy left with Jas J. Cannon
P.F. White, Shff

State of North Carolina }
Chowan County Court } December Term 1858

Ordered that James J. Cannon & William H Elliott be and they are hereby appointed a Patrol Committee for the upper District for the ensuing Year.
Wm R. Skinner, Clk

****

Patrol Order For W.S. Hedrick, Capt.
Aug. Term 1859

Executed by a Copy left with Wm. S. Hedrick, May 23rd 1859
P.F. White, Shff

State of North Carolina }
Chowan County Court } May Term 1859

Ordered that William S. Hedrick, John Roberts, Julian Gilliam, Peter M. Warren and Alexander Myers be and they are hereby appointed a Patrol for the District below Edenton, and that said Hedrick act as Captain thereof.
Issued the 11th day of May 1859
Wm R. Skinner, Clk

****

Patrol Order For Jos Moran & others
Feby Term 1859

Executed by a Copy left with Jos Moran Capt., Jany 4th 1859

Chowan County
Patrol Records

PF White, Shff

State of North Carolina }
Chowan County Court   } December Term 1858

Ordered that Joseph Moran, Charles Woodley, Aug R. Creecy, George Bond, David Small and John Bonner, be and they are hereby appointed a Patrol for below Edenton and Green Hall and that said Jos Moran act as Captain thereof.
Issued the 4th day of January 1859
Wm R Skinner, Clk

****

Patrol Order For Middle District
December Term 1858

Executed by leaving a Copy With E. Churchill Capt.
P.F. White, Shff

State of North Carolina }
Chowan County Court   } September Term 1858

Ordered that Ephraim Churchill, Jeremiah Evans, William Privitt Junr., William N. Bunch, and Thomas T. Leary be and they are hereby appointed a Patrol for the Middle District until the 1st April 1859 and that they act as a special Patrol from the 20th December to the 15th January next and that said Churchill act as Captain thereof.
Issued the 30th September 1858.
Wm R. Skinner, Clk

****

Patrol Order For Middle District
Novr Term 1859

Executed Aug. 13th
P.F. White, Shff

State of North Carolina }

Chowan County
Patrol Records

Chowan County Court } August Term 1859

Ordered that Ephraim Churchill, William N. Bunch, Jeremiah Evans, William Privitt Junr., & John W. Nowell be and they are hereby appointed a Patrol for the Middle District & that said Churchill act as Captain thereof.
Wm. R. Skinner, Clk

****

Patrol Order For Moses Hobbs et als
Feby Term 1861

Executed by a Copy left with Moses Hobs 17th Nov 1860
P F White, Shff

State of North Carolina }
Chowan County Court } Nov Term 1860

Ordered that Moses Hobbs, Thomas Pratt, Joseph Moran, Thomas C. Spruill, Augustus R. Creecy and John Newman be and they are hereby appointed a Patrol for the Upper portion of the District below Edenton, and that said Hobbs act as Captain of said Patrol.
Issued the 12th Nov 1860
Wm R Skinner, Clk

****

Patrol Order, Upper District For Wm. W. Ward
Nov Term 1859

Executed Aug 13th 1859
PF White, Shff

State of North Carolina }
Chowan County Court } August Term 1859

Ordered that William W. Ward, Jordan Hollowell, Jordan White, William G. Ward and Quinton Hollowell be and they are hereby appointed

Chowan County
Patrol Records

a Patrol for the Upper District and that said William W. Ward act as Captain thereof.
Issued 9th August 1859
Wm. R. Skinner, Clk

****

Patrol Order For West R. Leary et als
Febry Term 1861

Executed by a Copy left for W R Leary, Nov 17th 1860
PF White, Shff

State of North Carolina }
Chowan County Court } Nov Term 1860

Ordered that West R. Leary, John B. Satterfield, Lemuel Bunch, William Perry, Myles Ashley and Chas. S. Moore be and they are hereby appointed a Patrol for Rockahock District and that said Leary act as Captain thereof.
Issued the 12th Nov 1860
Wm R Skinner, Clk

****

Patrol Order, Rockyhock District
For John B. Satterfield & others
Feby Term 1860

Executed by a Copy left with John B Satterfield Nov 23rd 1859.
P.F. White, Shff

State of North Carolina }
Chowan County Court } November Term 1859

Ordered that John B. Satterfield, Charles Moore, West R. Leary, Joseph J. Byrum, William Leary and John Privitt be and they are hereby appointed Patrol for Rockyhock District and that said Satterfield act as Captain thereof.
Issued 14th Nov 1859

Chowan County
Patrol Records

Wm R Skinner, Clk

****

Patrol Order For Wm. Privitt Junr., & others
Febry Term 1860

Executed by Leaving a Copy at the residence of Wm. Privitt Junr., Capt., Nov 23rd 1859
P.F. White, Shff

State of North Carolina }
Chowan County Court } November Term 1859

      Ordered that William Privitt Junr., Ephraim Churchill, Jeremiah Evans, Benjamin L. Evans, John C. Pearce and William N. Bunch be and they are hereby appointed a Special Patrol for the Middle and Upper Districts and that they ride from the 15th of December 1859 to the 15th of January 1860 and that said Privitt act as Captain thereof.
Issued the 14th day of Nov 1859
Wm R Skinner, Clk

****

Patrol Order For A. J. Glover & others
Febry Term 1860

Executed by leaving a Copy with AJ Glover Capt.
P.F. White, Shff

State of North Carolina }
Chowan County Court } Nov Term 1859

      Ordered that A. J. Glover, George Bond, Joseph Copeland, William A. Gaskins and Thomas Smith be and they are hereby appointed a Patrol for Green Hall District and that A.J. Glover act as Captain thereof.
Wm. R. Skinner, Clk

****

Chowan County
Patrol Records

Patrol Order, Middle District
For Jeremiah Evans & others
Nov Term 1860

Executed by a Copy left for J. Evans Aug 18th 1860
PF White, Shff

State of North Carolina   }
Chowan County Court   } August Term 1860

    Ordered that Jeremiah Evans, Ephraim Churchill, Thomas J. Leary, Benj. L. Evans and John Churchill Junr., be and they are hereby appointed a Patrol for the Middle District and that said Jeremiah Evans act as Captain thereof.
Issued the 14th day of August AD 1860
Wm. R. Skinner, Clk

****

Patrol Order For Jordan White & others
Nov Term 1860

Executed by leaving a Copy with Jordan White Aug 18th 1860
P.F. White, Shff.

State of North Carolina   }
Chowan County Court   } Aug Term 1860

    Ordered that Jordan White, Jordan Hollowell, Quinton Hollowell, William G. Ward and Townsend E. Ward be and they are hereby appointed a Patrol for the Upper District and that said Jordan White act as Captain thereof.
Isued the 14th August AD 1860
Wm R Skinner, Clk

****

Patrol Order For Jeremiah Evans et als
Feby Term 1861

Chowan County
Patrol Records

Executed by a Copy left with Jeremiah Evans.
P.F. White, Shff

State of North Carolina }
Chowan County Court } Nov Term 1860

      Ordered that the regular Patrol for the Middle District be required to ride three nights in each week for the space of three weeks from the receipt hereof and as often thereafter as circumstances may require, and that William Leary be added to the Company.
Issued the 13th day of Nov 1860
Wm R. Skinner, Clk

****

Patrol Order, Green Hall
For Wm H Bonner et als
Feby Term 1861

Executed by a Copy left with Wm H. Bonner Capt., Nov 12th 1860
PF White, Shff

State of North Carolina }
Chowan County Court } Nov Term 1860

      Ordered that William H Bonner, Isaac Kale, William A. Gaskins, H.C. Thatch and Henry Mitchell be and they are hereby appointed a Patrol for Green Hall District, and that they be required to ride three nights in each week, for three weeks next ensuing the receipt hereof and there after as often as may be necessary, and that said Bonner act as Captain of said Patrol.
Issued 12th day of Nov 1860
Wm R Skinner, Clk

****

Patrol Order For Below Edenton
Aug Term 1861

Executed by a Copy left with Dr. Wm G. Leary May 6th 1861

Chowan County
Patrol Records

P.F. White, Shff

State of North Carolina }
Chowan County Court } May Term 1861

     Ordered that Wm. J. Leary, Elijah Smith[?], Wesley Ellis, Chas Woodley, Aug R. Creecy, Jos Moran, Geo H. Coke, Peter M Warren, Wm Hedrick, Jos T. Waff, C.G. Davenport, Watson White, Peter F. White, W.R. Shannonhouse, Nathail Woodward, Nathal Woodward Junr., John Long, John Higgins & John Bonner, John Goodwin be and they are hereby appointed a Patrol below Edenton that the said Wm Leary act as Captain thereof.
Wm. R. Skinner, Clk

****

Patrol Order For Wm H. Bonner
Aug Term 1861

Executed by a Copy left with Wm H Bonner May 16th 1861
PF White, Shff

State of North Carolina }
Chowan County } May Term 1861

     Ordered that the following persons be and they are hereby appointed Patrol for Green Hall District, to wit: Wm H Bonner, Wm A Gaskins, Geo Bond, Isaac Kale, James E. Evans, Thomas Smith, George Parker, William Davenport, Isaac Smith, Jos Copeland, John Bass, James Wilson, Jesse Davis, James Bonner, Wm Smith, Wm H. Smith, Samuel Eshon, Jesse Parker, Wm. W. Hall, Daniel Ward, Ephraim B Elliott and that Wm H Bonner act as Captain thereof.
Wm R. Skinner, Clk

****

Patrol Order For Julian Gilliam et als
Febry Term 1861

Executed by leaving a Copy with Jul Gilliam, Nov 17th 1860

Chowan County
Patrol Records

PF White, Shff

State of North Carolina }
Chowan County Court } Nov Term 1860

      Ordered that Julian Gilliam, William Hedrick, Joseph Mardie, George H. Coke, Peter M Warren and John Roberts be and they are hereby appointed a Patrol for the Lower Portion of the District below Edenton, and that said Gilliam act as Captain of said Patrol.
Issued the 12th day of Nov 1860
Wm R Skinner, Clk

****

Patrol Order Upper District For Jas J Cannon
Aug. Term 1861

Executed by leaving a Copy for James J Cannon
P.F. White, Shff

State of North Carolina }
Chowan County Court } May Term 1861

      Ordered that James J. Cannon, R.H. Winborne, Wm. H. Elliott, N.L. Cullins, H.H. Hobbs, Dossey Welch, Wm Deans, Andrew Ward, Starkey B. Evans, Martin L. Brinkley, Jos Spruill, and James Boyce be and they are hereby appointed a patrol for the upper District, and that they comply with the Law in every respect, and at the same time give information to some Magistrate of all suspicious persons in said District, and that said James J. Cannon act as Captain thereof.
Wm. R. Skinner, Clk

****

Patrol Order For Wm. H. Bonner, Green Hall Dist.
May Term 1861

Executed by a Copy left with Bonner Feb. 12th 1861
P F White, Shff

Chowan County
Patrol Records

State of North Carolina }
Chowan County Court } Feby Term 1861

Ordered that Thomas Smith, George Bond, and James E. Evans be and they are hereby appointed as a part of the Patrol in Green Hall District in the place of Henry C. Thatch and Henry Mitchell removed.
Issued 12th Feby 1861
Wm R Skinner, Clk

****

Patrol Order, Below Edenton
Aug. Term 1861

Executed by a Copy left with Dr. Wm J Leary may 7th 1961
P.F. White, Shff

State of North Carolina }
Chowan County Court } May Term 1861

Ordered that Dr. W. Leary be appointed Captain of the Patrol below Edenton and that he be authorized to enroll every man below Edenton, or any money or so many of them as he may think Proper and
Wm. R. Skinner, Clk

****

Patrol Order For Middle District
Jeremiah Evans, Capt.

Executed by a Copy left with Jer. Evans, May 6th 1861
P.F. White, Shff

State of North Carolina }
Chowan County Court } May Term 1861

Ordered that John H. Garrett, John A. Bunch, Jeremiah Evans, Thomas Evans, Thomas Cochrane Junr., John Churchill, Benj. L. Evans, Ephraim Churchill, Miles C. Brinkley, William Leary, Elisha Burke, John

Chowan County
Patrol Records

W. Newell & George Sutton be and they are hereby appointed a Patrol for the Middle District and that Jeremiah Evans act as Captain thereof
Wm. R. Skinner, Clk

****

Patrol Order, Below Edenton
May Term 1854, Chowan County Court
William Norcom Esq. & others

Executed by leaving a Copy of the within, with William Norcom
T.S. Hoskins, Shff

State of North Carolina }
Chowan County Court   } Febry Term 1854

Ordered that William Norcom, Joseph S. Leary, [?] D Louther Junr., Edmund Norcom and P. **[Faded]**, be and they are hereby appointed a Patrol Below Edenton, Company No 2 and that said William **[Faded]** as Captain thereof
Wm R Skinner, Clk

****

Patrol Order, Middle District
Febry Term 1862

Executed by a Copy left 17th Decr 1861
PF White, Shff

State of North Carolina }
Chowan County Court   } Nov Term 1861

Ordered that Henderson Simpson, Myles C. Brinkley and Thomas Evans be and they are hereby appointed a Patrol Committee for the Middle District

Wm R Skinner, Clk

****

Chowan County
Patrol Records

Patrol Order, Upper District
Febry Term 1862

Executed by a Copy left 17th

P.F. White, Shff

State of North Carolina }
Chowan County Court } Nov Term 1861

    Ordered that Richard Dillard, William H. Elliott and James J. Cannon be and they are hereby appointed a Patrol Committee for the Upper District
Wm R. Skinner, Clk

Chowan County
Bills of Sale

Chapter Six

Chowan County

Bills of Sale

North Carolina State Archives
Chowan County Records
Miscellaneous Slave Records
C.R.024.928.3

Know all Men by these Presents that I [Blank] of Chowan County in the Province of North Carolina, Planter, for & in Consideration of the sum of [Blank] to me in hand paid by Joshua Bodley of the County & Province aforesaid, Esquire, the receipt whereof, I hereby acknowledge, have bargained & Sold, and by these Presents do bargain & Sell, to the said Joshua Bodley, one Negro Man Slave, named [Blank] To have & to hold the said Negro Slave, to the said Joshua Bodley his Heirs, Executors, Administrators & Assigns forever, And I the said [Blank] for me my Heirs, Executors, & Administrators the said Negro Slave, to the said Joshua Bodley, his Executors, Administrators, will Warrant, & for ever Defend from the lawful Claim, of any Person or Persons whatsoever. In Witness whereof I have hereunto set my Hand & Seal the fourteenth Day of Novr. In the year of our Lord, One Thousand, Seven Hundred & Fifty Seven.

Chowan County
Bills of Sale

Signed Sealed & Delivered
In the Presence of [Blank]

****

Know all men By these Presents that I Miles Ellet of the County Chowan and State of No. Carolina for an Consideration of the Sum of one hundred pounds Currency to me in hand paid By Edmund Dunston whereof I do hereby acknowledge the Receipt and my self there with fully satisfied have bargained sold set over and Delivered in plain open market A certain Negro woman known by the Name of Sary and Child by the Name of Lucy which said Negroes I bind my self my heirs and Executors and assigns to make good the Rite and title of said Negroes to thee above Edmund Dunston his heirs and signs from me and my heirs or assigns for Ever ever in witness hereof I here unto set my hand and Seal this twenty fourth day of Feby Seventeen hundred and Ninety five.
Miles Elliott   (Seal)
Test. Luke Smithwick & Evan Simpson

State of No. Carolina   }
Bertie County   } May Term 1795

     The within Bill of sale from Miles Elliott to Edmund Dunston was proved in due form of law by the Oath of Luke Smithwick one of the subscribing Witnesses and Ordered to be Registered
Stevens Gray
Registered in the Bertie Registers Office, Book Q. page 364
Test David Turner, P. Register

****

Know all men by these presents that I Wm Felton of the County of Chowan and province of North Carolina for the Valluable Consideration of fifty six Pounds two Shillings and four pence States Currency to me in hand Paid have bargined and Sold and set over and Delivered unto Deliah Ming of the same County aforesaid one Negro boy named Mils Which negro I the said W. Felton will for Ever Warrant and Defend against the Lawfull Right or Clame of any person or persons What Ever unto the said Deliah Ming her heirs or assigns for Ever, In Witness Whereof I have here unto set my hand and seal this 2nd Day of October 1801.

Chowan County
Bills of Sale

John Sutton
William Felton   (Seal)

State of North Carolina   } Chowan County Court, December Term 1801

This Certifys that the within Bill of Sale was Exhibited in Open Court, and Acknowledged by William Felton & ordered to be Registered
Test Norfleet

I do hereby Certify that the within Bill of Sale was duly Registered in the Registers Office of the County aforesd this 7th day of April 1802 in Book R, No. 492 by
James Sutton, Regr.

****

Frederick Creecy To James Hoskins
Bill of Sale
Negroe Jim Registered the 14th Feby 1805 in Book B. page 125
James Sutton, Regr.

N Carolina   }
Chowan County }

Know all men by these Presents, that I Frederick Creecy of the County & State aforesaid for and in Consideration of the sum of Four Hundred & fifty dollars to me in hand Paid by James Hoskins of the County of Tyrell & State afforesaid, the Rect. Whereof I do hearby Acknowledge myself fully Satisfied Contented and Paid hath Bargained Sold and delivered and by these Presents do Bargain Sell and deliver unto him the said James Hoskins his Heirs and Assigns forever one Negroe Man by the Name of James of the age of Twenty one years, to have and to hold the aforesaid Negroe man free & clear from all manner of Incumbrance whatever, and I the said Frederick Creecy do for myself my Heirs Exrs, Admr & Assigns do forever Promise to Warrant the above named Negroe James from the Lawfull Claim of any Person or Persons whatever in witness whereof I have hearunto Set my hand & Seal this 8th day of October 1803.
Test. Fred Norcom
Fredk. Creecy   (Seal)

Chowan County
Bills of Sale

State of North Carolina }Chowan County Court
} September Term 1804

This Certifys that the within Bill of Sale was Exhibited in Court and duly proved by the Oath of Frederick Norcom & Ordered to be Registered
Test E. Norfleet

****

Deborah Taylor to Sarah Walton
Bill of Sale
Registered 18th Feby. 1805
In Book B Page 128
James Sutton, Regr.

State of N Carolina }
Chowan County }

Know all Men by these presents that I Deborah Taylor of County aforsd. For and in Consideration of the of the Natural Love and affection which I have and bear to my Daughter Sarah Walton of the County of Gates and State aforsd. And for divers other causes and Considerations hereunto moving have given, granted & Bargined and by these presents do give & grant unto the said Sarah Walton during her Natural life a certain Negro Woman by the Name of Rachel and her Increase, and after her death I give the said Negro Woman Rachel and Increase to my Grand Daughter Rebeckah Walton and in Case my Grand Daughter Rebeckah Walton should die without issue to return to the Taylor family To have and to hold unto the said Sarah Walton during her Natural life the aforementioned Negroe Woman Rachel and Increase And I the said Deborah Taylor all and singular the aforementioned Negroe woman Rachel and increase against the Claim or demand of any person will Warrant and Defend against the Claim of any person or persons whatever. In Witness Whereof I have hereunto set my hand and Seal this 12th Day of Septr. 1804
Signed Sealed and Delivered in the presents of:
Joseph C Benbury, Jurt.
     Her
Deborah X Taylor   (Seal)
     Mark

Chowan County
Bills of Sale

State of North Carolina } Chowan County Court
} September Term 1804

This Certifys that the above Deed of Gift was Exhibited in Court and Duly proved by the Oath of Joseph C. Benbury & Ordered to be Registered.
Test E Norfleet

****

William Blanchet, Bill of Sale
Registered this 5th day of August 1805
In Book B. Page 341
By James Sutton, Regr.

State of North Carolina
Chowan County

Know all men by these presents that I William Blanchet of Chowan County for & in consideration of one hundred pounds good and lawful money to me in hand paid by Abram Jordan at or before the Sealing and delivery of these presents the receipt whare of I the said William Blanchet I hareby acknowledged have granted, bargined and Sold and by these presents do grant bargin and sell unto the said Abram Jordan unto his ares and sins for ever one negro garl by the name of Selah, a slave and I the said William Blanchet for myself my ares executors and administrators To Warrant and for ever defend angast rite and title to the foresaid negro garl Selah unto Abram Jordan and his hares and assins forever and I the said William Blanchet do Warrant the fore said negro gearl Selah to be well [?] sound negro garl and so to remain at my [?] til I deliver her to Abram Jordan and if I don't deliver her I will pay the fore said Abram Jordan three [?] amount til I do deliver her and I the for said William Blanchet do agree to warrant and forever defend a good rite and titel to the fore said negro garl Selah unto the for said Abram Jordan and his ares and assins forever from all rites titels or demands from me and my ares or any person or persons laying of any clames or demands against the for said Negro garl Selah in witness that I have hare unto set my hand and fixt my seal the day and year above riten, May the fifthteenth day one thousand eight hundred and five, sind Seled and delivered in the presents of
Test Caleb C. Jordan
Test Elisabeth Ross, Jurt.

Chowan County
Bills of Sale

William Blanchet   (Seal)

State of North Carolina   } Chowan County Court
   } June Term 1805

This Certifys that the within Bill of Sale was exhibited in Court and duly proved by the Oath of Elizabeth Ross & Ordered to be Registered
Test E Norfleet

****

James Luten To James Jones
Bill of Sale, Negro boy Mike
9 Novr. 1812 by W. Jones
Registered in Book G. Page 55
By James Sutton, Regr.

State of North Carolina
Chowan County

Know all Men by these Presents that I James Luten of the County and State aforesaid, for and in Consideration of the sum of Two hundred Dollars and Fifty Cents to me in hand paid by James Jones of the County & State aforesaid I have this day sold and in open Market delivered to him the said James Jones a certain Negroe boy Called Mike, the receipt of the above sum I do hereby Warrant and forever defend the said Negroe boy Mike unto him the said James Jones his heirs Exors, Admors, & Assigns, against me my heirs, Exors. Admors. & assigns or against the claim or demand of any person or persons whomsoever.
    In Witness whereof I have hereunto set my hand & Seal this 9th day of November 1812.
Witness Fra Jones
Ja Sutton

State of North Carolina   }
Chowan County Court   } September Term 1814

The within Bill of Sale was exhibited in open Court on oath by Francis Jones and ordered to be registered
Will Norfleet, DC

Chowan County
Bills of Sale

****

Bill of Sale for Man George
1 Jany 1817, $700

State of North Carolina }
Chowan County }

Know all men by these Presents that I William Rombough of the County and State aforesaid, for and in Consideration of the Sum of Seven Hundred Dollars to me in hand paid by Edmd Hoskins of the Town of Edenton, County & State aforesaid the Receipt, whereof is hereby acknowledged have Granted bargained and Sold, and by these Presents do grant, bargain & Sell unto the said Edmd Hoskins, his heirs Executors and assigns, a Certain Negroe Man named George (a Slave) the title of which negro Slave Named George, I do hereby Warrant and defend against the claim or claims of all persons whatever, unto the said Edmd Hoskins, his heirs and Assigns for ever, In Witness Whereof I have hereunto set my hand and Seal 7th May 1817.
Wm. Rombough   (Seal)
Witness, Joseph Manning

****

Edenton 20th Aug. 1818, Recd from Wm. Jones Five Hundred Dollars, in full consideration for a certain negro girl slave named Maria, about eighteen years of age, sold him this day, and I do hereby Warrant and defend the right and title to the said negro to the said Wm. Jones, his heirs and Exors for ever, Witness my hand and seal the day and date above written
Signed Sealed & delivered in presents of [?]
Miles Wilder   (Seal)

****

Bill of Sale to Joseph Norcom, Esqr.

State of North Carolina }
Chowan County }

Chowan County
Bills of Sale

Know all Men by these presents that I William Badham Trustee of Lemuel P. Halsey of the County and State aforesaid, for and in Consideration of the sum of Seven hundred & Twenty Six Dollars in hand paid by Joseph Norcom of the County of Chowan at or before the ensealing and delivery of these presents the receipt whereof is hereby acknowledged, and he the said Joseph Norcom thereof and therefore and from every part thereof acquited, released, and discharged, have bargained Sold and delivered, and by these presents do bargain Sell and deliver unto the said Joseph Norcom, a certain Negro Woman Slave Named Eliza aged about Twenty Two Years, and her Two Children, John & Emily aged about three Years & fifteen Months.

To have and to hold the said Negro Slave Eliza and her Two Children John & Emily, unto him the said Joseph Norcom his executors, administrators and assigns forever, and I the said William Badham, shall and will Warrant and forever defend the right and Title of said Negro Slave Eliza and her Two Children John & Emily unto him the said Joseph Norcom his executors, administrators and assigns forever, against the Claims and demands of all and every person or persons whatsoever Claiming or to Claim by from or under Me and no further.

In Witness whereof I have hereunto set my hand and Seal this 11th Day of December A.D. 1848
Test
Wm Benbury
William Badham   (Seal)

****

$235

Twelve months after date with interest from date we promise to pay William A. Moore Clerk & Master in Equity on order Two hundred and thirty five dollars for purchase of slave Alfred -- Witness our hands and seals this 28th day of May 1859
John H. Hall   (Seal)
P F White   (Seal)

Chowan County
Free Persons of Color

Chapter Seven

Chowan County

Free Persons of Color

North Carolina State Archives
Chowan County Records
Miscellaneous Slave Records
C.R.024.928.3

Benja. Sanders Man Taffeys Certificate

North Carolina
Perq. County

This may Cartefy that the Bearer Hereof a Negro man named Ben is a free Negro as he formerly belonged to Mr. Jonathan Sharod Deceased who having Many Slaves & no Children alive not Desiering his Slaves Should Serve another Master Did in his Will Generously give them freedom Which if Disputed may be found on Record in the Court of the the said County aforesaid & the afore named Negro Man having a Desier to travel to Virginia to Seek better imployment we the Subscribers Do Cartify that the said Negro is a free man, has Ever Since his working for himself behaved Very honest therefore, we the Subscribers Do Recommend the

Chowan County
Free Persons of Color

Said to such Gentlemen as Shall imploy him. Witness our hands this 21 January 1774 [?] Ratlieff

****

Rec'd September 12th 1788 from William John Skinner One Negroe Woman Named Pations & a boy Child With her Said to be Manumitted by John Sanders Which Negroes ware Taken by said William J Skinner agreeable to the Act of Assembly provided Domestick Insurrections

****

Mr. William Littlejohn
Edenton
Feby the 10th 1802
Wm. Littlejohn Esqr.

Sir,

    I am Informed by Mr. Dominick that Eli Wilkins a person of Coulour In the Town of Edenton hath been taken up under Same of the Acts of Assembly & bound for his apearance to Chowan County Court at March Term 1802 where he is to Stand his Tryal for to be Sold as a Slave if My affidavit that I herewith forward to you is not suficient to Extricate the Sd. boy & for you to Give up the Recognizance of the Sd Dominick & let the Sd. boy Stand Discharged, I will forward any Other proof that may be deemed Necessary to that Efect as [?] able so to do: & Maye Also bound by the Laws of Nature & Humanity.

I Am with Submition
Your Hubl Servt.
Tamor Wilkins

State of North Carolina }
Martin County   }

Personally appeared before Me Ebenezer Slade one of the Justices for the County aforesaid Tamor Wilkins & Made Oath In Due form that on the Seventh of July one Thousand Seventeen Hundred & Eighty five She was

Chowan County
Free Persons of Color

Delivered of Male Child which She Called Eli Wilkins a Natural Born & Child of Coulour which Child after Coming of age to be bound She Bound as an Apprentice to one John Edwards of Bertie County who Some time Afterwards Removed to the then Cumberland Settlement & gave up the Indenture of Sd. Boy to his Sd. Mother, She then put the Sd. Boy with one John Acrey to learn the Hatters Trade, the Boy as She this Deponant Has since Understood Runaway from Sd. Acre, Better than Three years ago & as She has been Informed hath been Living with one Dominick since that time In the Town of Edenton which Sd. boy hath been brought to Her by the Sd. Dominick on the 10th Day of February one Thousand Eighteen Hundred & Two In the County & State aforesaid & she this Deponant Doth Acknowledge Sware him to be the Same boy, In Testimony whereof she this Deponant Hath put her hand & Declared the same.
   Tamer
Her + Mark
   Wilkins
Test, E Slade, JP for the County of Martin

Febry the 10th 1802 This May Certify that I have known the within mentioned Tamer Wilkins for Several Years & Believe there is no Doubt of her being free Born as will more fully apear By the Testimony of many in the County of Bertie if it should be Necessary, Given under My hand and Seal the day & Date above written
E Slade   (Seal)
Tamer Wilkins Affidavit

****

State of North Carolina   } February 17th 1844
Chowan County   }

Personally appeared before me, Thomas V Hathaway, Clerk of the Court of Pleas & Quarter Sessions, in and for said County, John Buchanan, a yellow man aged about thirty seven years; about five feet, six inches in height, & proved before me, by Duncan McDonald, of Edenton, that he was freeborn; that he was bound to said McDonald, until he arrived to the age of twenty one years, which time he served out: wherefore I do hereby Certify that the said John Buchanan hath made it, satisfactorily appear, that he is a free man & not a Slave & in testimony of his being a free man & no

Chowan County
Free Persons of Color

slave, as proved on oath, by said Duncan McDonald of Edenton, North Carolina -- I have hereto set my hand, & Seal of Office, at Edenton, the day & year aforesaid.

****

February Term 1851 County Court of Chowan

The Jurors for the State upon their oath present the following free negroes living in this County as having migrated into this the State of North Carolina contrary to the form of the Statute in such case made and provided viz.

Abram Savage, Dred Copeland, Agnis Brown, Henry Copeland, Alfred Folk, and June a girl living in Edenton with Thomas Miller.

It is therefore ordered by the Court that the Sheriff proceed immediately after the rising of this Court to notify the said free negroes that they must leave and go beyond the bounds of this State within twenty days next ensuing after the day upon which they shall be informed of this order, or they will be arrested by Warrant and carried before some Justices of the Peace of this County and bound over to appear at the next term of this Court to be dealt with according to law.

Test. Wm R. Skinner, Clk

Executed by delivering a Copy & making known the contents to June, Feby. 24th 1851. T.S. Hoskins, Shff. Executed on Abram Savage the 15th Feb 1851 by leaving a Copy of this Notice with him. Executed on Agnes Brown by a Coppy left - also on Alfred Folk by a Coppy left on the 20th Feb 1851. T.S. Hoskins, Shff. By P.F. White. Henry Copland not in this County.

Chapter Eight

Chowan County

Hiring of Slaves

North Carolina State Archives
Chowan County Records
Miscellaneous Slave Records
C.R.024.928.3

This Day Hired of Thos Godwin Junr., three Negro Slaves for which I promise and oblidge My Self my heirs Executors or Assigns to pay or cause to be paid to the Sd. Thos. Godwin Junr., or his Order the full Sum of three pound Eight Shillings in this province bills Pr. Month for every Month the Sd Godwin Shall Lett the Sd Negros Stay with me, & to Deliver the Sd Negros to the last Day of July Next Otherwise to for fitt and pay to the Said Godwin Or Order the Sum of four hundred pounds in this province bills, as witness my hand this 20th Day of April 1730

Witness Willm. Mackey
Filed ye 30th July 1730. J: A:

****

Chowan County
Hiring of Slaves

Joseph Hopkins Note £4

Nine Months after date I Promise to Mr. J. Pointer the Sum of Twenty four Pounds Specie for the hire of a Negroe Girl Calld Edney, as Witness my hand this 3rd April 1783
Joseph Hopkins
Witness, Robt. Miller

24th April Rec'd in part of the within note Thirty seven shilling and four pence. John Pointer

****

Note $25
E Devenport
25 $ with 3 1/2 months Interest making $25.43
Paid

Twelve Months after date, We or either of us, promise to pay Ann C Blount the Sum of Five Dollars, it being for the present years hire of Negro Woman Matilda & Child Mills. We bind ourselves, our heirs, executors, administrators and assigns to comply with all the terms of hiring said Negro. Given under our hands and seals, this the 2nd day of January 1852.
Ephraim Davenport   (Seal)
[Name Faded]   (Seal)

****

W. Grist & Allen Grist
Note for $200 for hire of Jaspar for 1855

On the first day of January 1856 either or each of us Promise to pay Dr. John Forcom, or Order Two Hundred Dollars for the hire of a negro boy Jaspar -- said boy to be furnished with necessary clothing & returned to Edenton the 1st of January 1856.
Jan 1st 1856
William Grist
Allen Grist   (Seal)

****

Chowan County
Hiring of Slaves

Jas Evans Note, $25.00

Paid by Ad[?], Feb 15th 1861
$40.18

    On the first day of Jany next we or either of us promise to pay Wm G Hancock the Sum of Twenty five dollars for the hire of Woman Rose, said Negro to be furnished with the usual quota of Clothing from the time of hiring, She is to be returned to Edenton on the 1st day of Jany, 1861, Witness our hands & Seals this June 1st 1861.
Jas. E Evans   (Seal)

****

Amount of Bacon due Mrs. Gaskins by Dave Gaskins for hire of **[Faded]** for 1866 - 40 4 1/2 to 1st of Nov 1866

4.1 2 1/2 Up To Nov the 11th
No of Bbl of Corn borrowed for the Year 1866, 20 BBls

Chowan County
Division of Slaves

Chapter Nine

Chowan County

Division of Slaves

North Carolina State Archives
Chowan County Records
Miscellaneous Slave Records
C.R.024.928.3

[No Date]
Division of Slaves between
Jane Henderson & Carolina Henderson

Lot No 1
Granville	950
Napoleon	600
Michel & 2 Children	1400
Minerva & Infant	1200
Caroline & Infant	1200
	5350

Lot No 1 Assigned to Jane Henderson and we direct that she pay over to Caroline Henderson Seventy five Dolls

Chowan County
Division of Slaves

Lot No 2	
Augustus	1000
Charles	650
Delsey & 2 Children	1500
Henry	800
Alesthia	600
George	250
Milly	100
	5600
Less Jack & Isbel	400
	5200

****

Mills Hill & Wife
Petition to the Court for sale
& Division of Negro
Copy to be served on John Williamsom
December Term 1817, Executed
John McCotter, Depty Shff

State of North Carolina } Court of Pleas & Quarter Sessions
Chowan County } September Term 1817

    The petition of Mills Hill and his Wife Sarah, to the Worshipfull the Justices of the County aforesaid

    Humbly complaining sheweth unto your Worships, that by virtue of a Deed of Gift, dated on the fifteenth day of February, in the Year of our Lord one thousand and eight hundred, executed by Sarah Simpson, to her four children, William Simpson, Robert Simpson, Dempsey Simpson and Sarah Simpson, the right and property in and to a certain negro woman named Rachel vested in the aforesaid William Simpson, Robert Simpson, Dempsey Simpson, and your petitioners, upon the death of the aforenamed Donor which happened on or about the [Blank] day of [Blank] 1817 -- your petitioners, Mills & Sarah, one of the aforenamed Donors having previously intermarried -- Your petitioners further shew unto your Worships that sometime on or about the [Blank] day of [Blank] and One thousand eight hundred and [Blank] the other donor William, Robert, and Dempsey, sold their right of the aforesaid negro to John Williamson, who

Chowan County
Division of Slaves

thereby became entitled to three undivided shares of her value; your petitioners being entitled to the other share, to Wit, one fourth part -- Your petitioners further shew, that they are desirous that the aforesaid negro should be sold so as to make a division - May it therefore please your Worships to order and direct that the aforesaid negro woman Rachel be sold at public Auction after due advertisement by the Sheriff upon such terms as to your Worships seem meet, and that one fourth of the nest proceeds be paid over to your petitioners -- And as in duty bound Your Petitioners will ever pray &c.
Mala Haughton
Solicitor

State of North Carolina } December Term 1817
Chowan County Court }

Mills Hill }
To } Petition to Sell a Negro and make Division
The Court }

    Ordered, That the Sheriff of the County aforesaid, sell at public sale, on a credit of Six months, giving twenty days public notice of the time of sale, the Negro Woman mentioned in the petition, named Rachel; and that distribution take place pursuant to the prayer of the said Petition, and that report thereof be made by next Term.
Test. Henry Wills, Dep. Clk

****

We the Subscribers having met agreeably to the annexed order, do report that upon examination of the property, find it impracticable to make an equitable division without a sale of the Negroes, Which is respectfully Submitted, Edenton 15th March 1819
[?], M. R. Sawyer, Jas R Burt[?], JR Ca[?]

****

          John Wyatt et als to the Court
          Petition for sale of a Negroe
          To be Served on Mrs. Sarah Whipple

Chowan County
Division of Slaves

& returned to Court
Executed by leaving a Copy of this Petition
With Sarah Whipple 15th June 1831
Wm D Rascoe, Shff

State of North Carolina }
Chowan County Court   } March Term 1831

   To the Worshipful Justices of said County, The Petition of John Wyatt & his Wife Sarah, & of Robert Keating Junr., by his Father and next friend, Robert Kealing, Humbly Sheweth unto your Worships, that your petitioners & Sarah Whipple of said County are Tenants in Common of a Negroe Man Slave, named Harry of about 58 years of age, that no Division can be made of said Negro without a Sale, and your Petitioners, are desirous that a Sale should be made for that purpose, Your Petitioners therefore pray that a Copy of this Subpa. & writ issue to said Sarah Whipple, Commanding her to appear, before your Worships, to shew Cause why a Sale should not be made and your Petitioners Pray, a Sale may be made & the Proceeds devided, and as in duly bound &c.
Malachi Haughton, Atto for Petrs.

Rec'd Edenton, 1st November 1832 from Edmund Hoskins Clerk of the County Court of Chowan Twenty Six Dollars 38/100 in full for my proportion of the Sale of Negroe Harry, Sold under a Decree of the Court, it being one half of the Amt. After deducting the Cost
$26.38/100
Sarah Whipple

Edmund Hoskins Esquire, Clerk of Chowan County Court
   Sir, be pleased to pay to Richard Howett my share or distributive part of the proceeds of negro Man Harry, sold by virtue of a Petition to Chowan County Court to make a division between myself, my sister and Mrs. Whipple and his receipt shall be your discharge -- I being now of full age, Witness my hand the 20th October 1832. Say $13.19
Test. Robert Keating Junr.

Chowan County
Division of Slaves

Rec'd Edenton 9th December 1833 from Edmund Hoskins, Clk of Chowan County Court, thirteen dollars 19/100 in full for my Wifes proportion of the Sale of Negroe Man Harry (deducting the Cost) sold according to a Decree of said Court at September Term 1831.
John B. Wyatt

Clk for Peto	20
Subp	50
3 Cont.	90
Commrs and Sale	3.08
	4.68
Shff	30
Atto MH	4.00
	8.98

****

Sandford E Goodwin & wife & others to the Court
Petition for Division of Slaves
Filed at Nov Term 1839

Freeholders: William R Skinner, Henderson Simpson, Baker F Welch, Wm. Bratton & Wm. H Elliott or any three of them

State of North Carolina } Court of Pleas & Quarter Sessions
Chowan County } November term 1839

  To the worshipfull Justices of said Court - the Petition of Sandford E Goodwin & his Wife Penelope and of Caleb Goodwin and his Wife Esther Ann Goodwin - Humbly sheweth unto your Worships that your petitioners are tenants in common of the following negro Slaves to wit, Woman Mary and children Bob and Andrew & also an infant child of said Mary, Man Isaac, girl Hester and girl Amy - your petitioner Sandford E Goodwin in right of his wife Penelope being entitled to one individual half of said slaves and your Petitioner the said Caleb Goodwin in right of his wife Esther Ann being entitled to the other individual half of said slaves and your Petitioners are desirous to have a division of said slaves: they therefore pray your Worships to appoint three freeholders to divide

Chowan County
Division of Slaves

said slaves as nearly co-equally as possible and that your Worships may have such other and further relief as to your Worships shall seem meet; and as in duty bound your Petitioners will ever pray &c.
Malachi Haughton, Solr. For Petitioners.

State of North Carolina }
Chowan County Court } November Term 1839

Ordered, that William R. Skinner, Henderson Simpson, Baker F. Welch, William Bratten and William H. Elliott, Esquires, be appointed Commissioners to divide the negroes between Sandford E. Goodwin & Wife Penelope and Caleb Goodwin and Wife Easther Ann, as prayed for, or any three of them to Act and make report.
Issued 27th Decr. 1839
Test. John Bush, Clk
By T.V. Hathaway, Dpty Clk

Pursuant to the above order the commissioners after being duly sworn have proceeded to allot and divide the Negroes set forth in this report between the persons set forth in the above order in following manner, Lot No 1, Mary & child Silas valued at 600 dollars, Boy Bob valued at 225 dollars, Boy Andrew valued at 150 dollars. To Caleb Goodwin and wife Esther Ann Lot No 2, Man Isaac valued at 700 dollars, girl Hester valued at 200 dollars, Girl Amey 175 dollars, to Sandford E Goodwin and wife Penelope they paying to Lot No 1, Fifty dollars all of which is respectfully submitted Jany, 4th 1840

Wm Bratton   (Seal)
Wm. R. Skinner   (Seal)
Henderson Simpson   (Seal)
William H. Elliott (Seal)

****

[Editor's note: This document was part of a Civil law suit brought on by a Petition to divide Slaves]

Officers
Fi Fa

Chowan County
Division of Slaves

Emanuel Walker & wife et als
August Term 1841
W.D. Rascoe, Shff

State of North Carolina
To the Sheriff of Chowan County, Greeting:
We Command you, that, That of the goods and chattels, lands and tenements of Emanuel Walker, & wife Mary B., Mary F. Nixson, William Nixson, Thomas M. Nixson and Erasmus Nixson [if to be found in your bailiwick] you cause to be made the sum of Twenty three dollars and Ninety five cents which was lately in our County Court of Pleas and Quarter Sessions held for Chowan County, at the Court House in Edenton, adjudged against them in their Petition of Emanuel Walker & wife & Thos M. Carter & others for division of Negroes for cost and charges in the said suit expended, whereof the said Emanuel Walker & wife, Mary F., Thos. M., William & Erastus Nixson are liable as to us appears of record. And have you the said monies before the Justices of our said Court on the first Monday in August next, then and there to render to the Officers of the Court their costs and charges aforesaid. Herein fail not, and have you then and there this writ. Witness, John Bush, Clerk of our said Court at Edenton, the first Monday in May in the 65th year of our Independence, Anno Dom. 1841.
Issued 5th day of June 1841
John Bush, Clk
By T.V. Hathaway, Dpty Clk

Clk	$12.95
Shff	3.00
Atto M H	4.00
Dr. G.W. B. for Answer of Child	4.00
	$23.95

****

William Coffield & others to the Court
Petition to sell Slaves

Chowan County
Division of Slaves

Begs leave to report that after due Notice did sell on a Credit of Six Months with interest after date, on the 1st January 1846 -- the following Negro Slaves, to wit:

Woman Mary & Child Daniel	} to Jon. Coffield	$540
Girl Cherry	} ditto	150
Do Isabell	}	180
Man Toney	} Wm J. Holley	645
		$1515

By 2/2 Per ct Coms	37.88	
Cost to Clerk	1.96	
A.J. Turner for bringing Negroe to town	1.00	
Atto Heath	4.00	44.84
		$1460.16

****

James Woodward & others to the Court
Petition to sell Slaves
Filed Nov. Term 1853
Prayer granted; Wm. H. Harrell directed to sell
See Decree within

State of North Carolina }
Chowan County }

 To the worshipful the Justices of the Court pf Pleas and Quarter Sessions for the said County, Nov. Term 1853

 The petition of James Woodward, in right of his wife Maria, and of Joseph Henry Harrell and Mary Elizabeth Harrell, infants of tender years, by their Guardian, William H. Harrell, respectfully showeth unto your Worships that they are tenants in common in two slaves, to wit: One named Joe, and the other named Jim; and that each one of your petitioners desires to have his and her share of said Slaves in severalty, which they cannot have by an actual division thereof: but may have by a sale and division of the proceeds. Your Petitioners therefore, pray that your Worships will appoint some suitable person to make sale of said slaves, in such manner and upon such terms, as your Worships may deem best, and

Chowan County
Division of Slaves

who shall make a report of his proceedings to the next term of this Court; and that your Worships will make such other and further Orders as may be necessary, Inst and proper.

And as bound, they will ever pray &c

W.F. Riddick, Solicitor for petitioners.

State of North Carolina }
Chowan County }

By a decree of this Court at Nov Term 1853, Petitioners James Woodward & others have sold before the Court House door in this County the negroes pursuant to said Order, Namely Boy Joe at One thousand thirty one dollars & Boy Jim at One thousand dollars, Andrew J Glover being the purchaser of boy Jim & Henry A Bond the purchaser of Boy Joe. The amounts of cost of petition &c being seven dollars & eighty cents - being deducted from the whole amount leaving a balance of Two Thousand and twenty three 20/100 dollars which I respectfully submit.

William H. Harrell, Commissioner, $6.00.

Petition	.50
Copy do	.50
Decree	.40
Copy do	.40
1 Cont	.30
determ	.75
Report	.75
	3.60
order	.20
	3.80
Atto	4.00
	7.80

****

Robt Beasly & others to the Court
Ptn sale of Slaves for division
To February Term 1854

State of North Carolina } Court of Pleas & Quarter Sessions

Chowan County
Division of Slaves

Chowan County } February Term 1854

To the worshipfull, the Justices of said Court: The petition of Robert Beasly, Joseph Bunch in right of his wife Rebecca, and Augustus R. Creecy, an infant under the age of twenty one years, by his Guardian, Thomas H. Leary Junr., respectfully sheweth unto your Worships, that they are tenants in common of certain slaves to wit, negro woman Esther and her children.

Your Petitioners further show, that they desire to have to have the said Slaves divided among them according to their respective rights and interests in the same, but that a division in kind cannot be made without injury to the parties concerned. Your petitioners therefore pray your Worships order a sale thereof, on such terms as to your Worships may seem best, and that the proceeds of the sale may be divided among them according to their respective rights and interests in said slaves. And Your Petitioners, as in duty bound will ever pray&c.
Leary, Solr., pro Petitioners

Robt. Beasly & als to the Court
Decree

Robert Beasly & als to the Court
Ptn for sale of Slaves
February Term 1854

It appearing after satisfaction of the Court that the Petitioners in the above case are tenants in common of the Slaves cannot be divided in kind among the parties interested, it is Therefore ordered adjudged and decreed that Jno C. Badham Esqr be appointed commissioner to make sale of said slaves, and it is further ordered that after advertisement of the sale at the Court House door, in the Town of Edenton and at three or more public places in theCounty of Chowan, for twenty days, he proceeded to sell the said slaves at the Court House aforesaid, to the highest bidder at public auction upon a credit of six months with interest from date, and that he take bonds with approved Security for the payment of the purchase money - and it is further ordered that said commissioner make his return to the next Term of this Court.

Chowan County
Division of Slaves

Report
Recorded in Book B., Page 207 & 208

State of North Carolina
Chowan County

To the Worshipful, the Justices of the Court of Pleas and Quarter sessions May Term 1854.

In obedience to an order of said Court at Feb. term last I John C. Badham Commissioner appointed by the Court for that purpose, after giving due notice, proceeded, on the 10th day of April at Edenton, to expose to public sale the following property, viz: negro woman Esther and her two young children, heretofore held in common by Robert Beasley, Augustus Creecy, and Joseph Bunch in right of his wife Rebecca on a credit of six months, according to the order of the Court: where and when Mills Roberts became the purchaser at the price of twelve hundred dollars: Whereupon, he, the said Roberts Executed to me a bond with good security for the purchase money according to the terms of sale, and took full possession of the said property - All of which is respectfully submitted.
J.C. Badham, Commissioner.

****

Williamson Goodwin & Isabella M. White to the Court
Petn. for sale of Slaves for Division
To Novr. Term 1854

State of North Carolina   } Court of Pleas & Quarter Sessions
Chowan County   } November Term 1834

To the Worshipfull, the justices of said Court:
The Petition of Williamson Goodwin and wife Mary in right of said Mary, and Isabella M. White an infant under twenty one years of age Respectfully sheweth to your Worships, that they are tenants in common of a certain negro Slave Stephen.
    Your petitioners further show that they desire to have the said Slave divided between them according to their respective rights and interests in the same, but that a division in kind cannot be made to the parties concerned - Your petitioners therefore pray your Worships to order

Chowan County
Division of Slaves

a sale thereof on such terms as to your Worships may deem best; and that the proceeds of the sale may be divided among them according to their respective rights and interests in said Slave. Your petitioners firther show that petitioner Isabella M. is a minor and without a guardian, they therefore pray Your Worships to appoint some suitable person Guardian ad litem to represent her rights and interests in this case and your Petitioners, as in duty bound will ever pray &c.
T.H. Leary Junr., Solr. Pro petitioners

Prayer Granted
On motion W.R. Skinner was appointed guardian ad Litem for Isabella M. White, P.F. White, Commissioner

---

W. Goodwin, Wife & als to the Court
Order of Sale

Williamson Goodwin, Wife & als }
To the Court }
Order of Sale }

It appearing to the satisfaction of the Court that the Petitioners are tenants in common of the slave named in the petition and that the said Slave cannot be divided in kind among the parties interested, it is therefore ordered, adjudged, and decreed, that C.F. White be appointed Commissioner to make sale of said Slave and it is further ordered that after advertisement of the sale at the Court House door, in the Town of Edenton, and at three or more public places in the County of Chowan, for at least twenty days he proceeded to sell said Slave, at the Court House aforesaid, to the highest bidder, at public auction upon a credit of six months with interest, first taking bond with approved security for the payment of the purchase money. It is further ordered that said Commissioner make his return to the next Term of this Court.

Williamson Goodwin & wife & als to the Court
Decree
Clk Petition $0.40

Chowan County
Division of Slaves

It appearing to the satisfaction of the Court that the purchase money in this has been paid to the Commissioner amounting to the sum of Eleven hundred and ten dollars. It is therefore ordered, adjudged and decreed, that the said Commissioner, after first paying the costs of this suit and also deducting the sum of fifty five dollars and fifty cents, and thirteen dollars and twenty five cents expenses incurred in apprehending and safely keeping the negro mentioned in the petition in this case, which is hereby allowed to him upon the sale and report, proceed to dispose of the residue thereof as follows, To Wit: one half to petitioner Williamson Goodwin in right of his wife Mary, and the other half to the other petitioner Isabella M. White.

State of North Carolina } Court of Pleas and Quarter Sessions
Chowan County   }

To William R Skinner Guardian Ad Litem of Isabela M White Greeting:
For certain causes offered before our Court of Pleas and Quarter Sessions, for the County of Chowan, we command and enjoin you the said William R. Skinner that laying all other matters aside, and notwithstanding every excuse, you personally appear before the Justices of the Court of Pleas and Quarter Sessions next, to answer concerning those things which shall then and there be objected to you, in and by the Petition of Williamson Goodwin et als to the Court. And further to do and receive what our said Court shall then and there consider in this behalf. And this you shall in no wise omit, under the penalty by Law enjoined. Witness, William R. Skinner, Clerk of said Court at Edenton, the First Monday of Nov Anno Dom., and in the 79th year of our Independence.
Wm R Skinner, Clk

Account for Expenses of the sale of man Stephen. Paid John Hall & Oliver Sund[?] for Jail fees — $7.25
Paid Jos. G Godfrey for going to look for said boy — 4.00
My expences to Plymouth for the same purpose — 2.00
Commissioners 5 P Cent — 55.50
Whole Amt. — $68.75

Clk Petition   .40

Chowan County
Division of Slaves

Copy	.40
1 subpoena	1.00
Order appointing Guardian	.20
1 Cont.	.30
Order of Sale	.20
Determ	.75
Decree	.50
Report	.75
	$4.50
Atty Leary	4.00
	8.50

****

[Editor's note: This document is a fragment.]

Rea & others to the Court } Report to Fall Term 1854

The Undersigned, to whom it was referred to report on the expediency of selling the negroes mentioned in the Petition, begs leave to report that the testimony taken by him shews the Slaves to be unruly, and insubordinate, and that there is great danger of the Petitioners losing every year the profits which should arise from their labor in consequence of their vicious conduct. The Undersigned therefore reports that a sale of them would benefit the Petitioners.
Respectfully Submitted
Th: C. Manning
C V [?], CC

****

Townsend Wright, Trustee et als to the Court
Petition & Order for division of Slaves
From P.F. White, Shff

Chowan County Court of Pleas & Quarter Sessions
Febry Term 1857

To the Worshipful the Justices of the said Court, the Petition of Townsend Wright, Trustee of Mary C. Foxwell, of Richard Henrys Wife Justina A.,

Chowan County
Division of Slaves

of Henry White and Wife Althea showeth, that they are tenants in common, in equal proportion of the following Slaves to wit: Patty, Galvin, Emily, Lucinda, William, Bryan, Alonzo, Roxilla, Cannon & Miles, said Wright being entitled to one third of the same in right of said Mary Foxwell to be held in trust for her, agreeable to a Trust Deed to him, of record in Chowan County said Richard Henry and Wife Justina A. to one third in right of said Justina A, and said Henry White and wife Althea to one third of the same, in right of said Alethea.

Petitioners further show your Worships, that they are unwilling longer to remain tenants in Common, but on the contrary said Wright, in right of said Mary & said Richard Henry and wife Justena & and said Henry White and wife Althea, are desirous that the Share of each as aforesaid should be assigned according to their interests respectively.

They therefore pray, that Partition be decreed in manner and form as aforesaid, and that Commissioners be appointed to divide. Allot, and report accordingly: and that they have such other and further relief as by Act or Acts of Assembly, in such Cases made and provided is allowed

Heath, Solr.

On motion the following freeholders, to Wit: T.L. Skinner, James D Wynn, T. W. Hudgins, A.J. Glover, James N. Floyd and John H. Hall or any three of them and a Justice are appointed commissioners to divide the Slaves named in the petition into three equal shares, and to allot to each of the petitioners one share thereof, in severalty, and to report their proceedings in due form of law to the next term of this Court
Wm. R. Skinner, Clk

Division of negroes between Townsend Wright Trustee of Mary C. Foxwell - Richard Henry & Wife Justina A -- and Henry White and Wife Althea

Patty valued at	350
Galvin	900
Emily	700
Lucinda & Children	1250
Alonzo, Roxanna & Cannon	
William valued at	600
Bryan	500

Chowan County
Division of Slaves

On motion the following freeholders, to wit: T.L. Skinner, JP, James D. Wynn, JP, T.W. Hudgins, A.J. Glover, James N. Floyd, and John H. Hall or any three of them and a Justice, are appointed Commissioners to divide the Slaves named in the Petition into equal shares, and allot to each of the petitioners one share thereof in severalty, and to report their proceedings in due form of law to the next term of the Court.
Wm R. Skinner, Clk

Division of Negroes between Richard Henry & Wife Justina A. & of Henry White & Wife Althea

Jim valued at	$500
Valentine valued at	$1200
Bob valued at	$1050
Caroline & Children Mary & Tom	$1300
	$4050
Half of which	$2025

Lot 1st
Caroline, Mary & Tom	$1300
Jim	$500
	$1800

Lot 2nd
Valentine	$1200
Bob	$1050
	$2250

The Committee undersigned having examined the above lot of negroes have divided them into two lots as ordered by the Court and report that the only proper division makes Lot 1 valued at $1800
Lot 2 valued at $2250
Leaving a difference of $450 the half of which or $225 must be paid by the drawer of Lot No 2 to Lot No 1

The Committee further deside that Richard Henry & Justina A. shall take Lot No 1, and that Henry White & Althea shall take Lot No 2 and pay to the holders of Lot No 1 the sum of $225.

Chowan County
Division of Slaves

To 1800	Lot 1	
Add 225		
$2025		

From 2250	Lot 2	
Deduct 225		
$2025		

The signers of this report were qualified for their duty by oath before me and signed the report in my presence.
Feb 11th 1857, T.L. Skinner, JP
T.W. Hudgins, J.N. Floyd & John H. Hall

****

John Thompson et als to the Court
Petition to Sell Slaves for Division
Recorded in Report C, Page 39
Feb. Term

State of North Carolina   } Court of Pleas & Quarter Sessions
Chowan County   } Feb Term 1860

  The Petition of John Thompson, Samuel N Burill[?], William Johnson, Thomas Johnson, & Ann Ramsay, respectfully showeth unto your Worships, that they are tenants in common of certain slaves, to wit, Malvina and child William & boy Joe - your petitioners further show that they desire to have the said Slaves divided among them according to their respective rights & interests in the same, but that a division in kind cannot be made without injury to the parties concerned.

  Your Petitioners therefore pray your Worships to order a sale thereof on such terms as to Your Worships shall seem best, and that the proceeds of the sale may be divided among them according to their respective rights, and interests in said Slaves.

  And Your Petitioners as in duty bound will ever pray.
J.C. Badham, Atty

Chowan County
Division of Slaves

John Thompson et als to the Court
Petition to Sell Slaves for partition

In obedience to the order in the above case the undersigned proceeded on the 10th day of April 1860 to sell the slaves named in the petition, at public auction at the Court House door in Edenton, after due advertisement on a credit of six months with interest, when and where John H. Hall appeared and bid for said woman Malvina & child the sum of one thousand five hundred dollars. And Ann Ramsay appeared and bid for said boy Joe the sum of three hundred & ninety Six dollars they being the last and highest bidders, said Slaves were struck off to them at the prices aforesaid. All of which is respectively submitted.

Wm. R. Skinner, Commr.

Petition	25
3 Cont	90
Determ	75
Order	20
	2.10
Report	75
	2.85
Atty Badham	4.00
	$6.85

Chowan County
Miscellaneous Records

Chapter Ten

Chowan County

Miscellaneous Records

North Carolina State Archives
Chowan County Records
Miscellaneous Slave Records
C.R.024.928.3

Doctor Beasely & Doctor Ram[?]

Rose, a Woman, 38 years, has Child 1 year & 1/2 at ye breast

Suke, a Woman, 22 years, 3 Months gone wt. Child

Rachael, a Girl, 18 years, has a Sucking infant

Dick, a Man, 25 years, in health

John, a Boy, 10 years ditto

Sam, a Boy, 7 years, ditto but weakly

Chowan County
Miscellaneous Records

Tom, a Boy, 5 years, ditto in health but delicate

Elliot, a Boy, 1 year, ditto the same

Harry, a Boy, 1 year, Sickly & tender

Jenny, a Girl, 3 years, in Health but delicate

Milly, a Girl, 2 years, in health

Herriot
Child of Rachael, a Girl, 6 months, Fat & in health

Maria, a Girl, 1 year, in health & delicate

Nancy, a Girl, 1 year, in health

Ned, a Boy, 14 years, in health

Eliza Hamilton, Polly Custis, Jas Boyce
Names of my Household

****

Sandy, Phillip, Daniel & Guy, belonging to Richard Brownrigg

Godfrey, Randolph, Washington & Dave, Belonging to Charles E. Johnston

Lewis belonging to Samuel Simpson
Sam belonging to Benj. White
Catoe belonging to Edward S Waff
Liah & Ned belonging to Exum Simpson
Isaac belonging to Josiah Spivey
Ben " Miles Welch
Jim " David Small
Harry belonging to John Bonner
Isaac & Nat belonging to William Smith

Chowan County
Miscellaneous Records

Peter belonging to John Felton

****

Account Sales of Negroe
H. Gregory, Estate
March 1800

Account Sales of a Negroe boy Abraham sold at Public Vendue at six months Credit.

Chowan County 10th February 1798
Negroe boy Abraham
To lot Estiole[?] £100
£97.10.0
Chas Roberts, Sherif
E Ea[?]

****

A. Rodrigue & Honore Neil to the Governor
Bond

North Carolina   } Ss.
County of Chowan   }

Know all Men by these presents that we A. Rodrigue & Honore Neil are held & firmly bound unto Richard Dobbs Speight Esqr. Governor of the State & his successors in Office in the sum of One thousand Pounds Current Money of the said State: To which payment well & truly to be made, we bind ourselves jointly & severally our & each of our heirs, Exrs. & Admrs firmly by these presents given at Edenton this 1st Day of August 1795.

The Condition of the above obligation is such that whereas the above bounden A. Rodrigue of the Island of St. Domingo last from Norfolk in the State of Virginia hath imported by land into this State a certain Negroe fellow called Francis lately of the Island of St. Domingo contrary to the Laws of this State: Now -- this Obligation Witnesseth & it is true intent &

Chowan County
Miscellaneous Records

meaning thereof that if the said A. Rodrigue shall well & truly & as soon as may be carry out of this State the said Negroe Francis & shall not offer to sell or dispose of the said Negroe, so long as he stayeth or remaineth in this State then this Obligation to be Void & of no effect otherwise to remain in full force & virtue.
Sealed & Delivered In the Presence of
Michl: Payne & Myles Omally
A. Rodrigue   (Seal)
H. Neil   (Seal)

****

Mr. Richard Hoskins
Care of Mr. Edmund Hoskins, Mercht.
Edenton, June 1805

Dear Richard,   Martin June 5th
    You Must Try and Sell Your Possessions to Live, as it is Out of My Power to Sell the Lands you Purchased.
    You Must Talk Verry Sweet to the people that we bought Negroes off & Tell them that they shall have the Money Next Winter, Tell Mr Norfleet not to Make himself uneasy as he shall be certain of the Money in January.
    I shall goe Out in the Winter & shall Want you to goe with me, the Old Gentt is a Trying To Sell his Lands, as he is Determined to Move
    I wish you to give me answer what you can do Whether you are in a likely Way To Sell or not.
    My Complement To the Family
I am yours Sincere
Willis Wiggins
N.b. Mr. Lan[?] Williams is Dead

R. Hoskins Notes

Received of Baker Wiggins Two notes, One on Mr Wright for One Hundred & fifty Six Dollars thirty seven cents, & the other, on William

Chowan County
Miscellaneous Records

Wright for Sixty nine Dollars Seventy five cents, Which notes I promise To Pay -- they are due now
2 April 1805

Richard Hoskins Note
$323.88
Lewis Savoy

On or before the first day of January Eighteen Hundred & Seven I promise to Pay Lewis Savoy or order Three Hundred Twenty Three Dollars Eighty Eight Cents, for Value Received. Witness My hand 2 April 1805
Richard Hoskins   (Seal)

Baker Wiggins
29 May 1805

Received of Baker Wiggins One Hundred Dollars Which I promise To Pay & Take up a note of His Which Baker Hoskins holds for ninety One Dollars and the Balance Pay To Miles Hassell
Apl. 1st 1805

Wiggins Papers
$590.83

Copy of Sales of Negroes Bot. By Willis Wiggins & Richard Hoskins 1st Jany 1805

1. Boy Sheppard to Willis Wiggins	£131: 10
2. Girl Nan to Willis Wiggins	154.5
3. Boy Lindsy to Willis Wiggins	184.5
	£470
4. Girl Bett to Richard Hoskins	137
5. Girl Dilla to Richard Hoskins	126
6. Do. Bid off by W. Wiggins ready money	113 £847

Negroes Sold by Willis Wiggins
Boy Sheppard bid off at   £131:10:0   } due 1st July 1805

Chowan County
Miscellaneous Records

Girl Nan	154.5	} due 1st July 1805
Boy Lindsy	184.5	} due 1st July 1805
Williamsons Boy Ben	137:5:0	due 10 Apl 1805
Girl Kate	150:0:0	due 18 Feby 1805
Interest on do		173
Bal. Boy George Wm. Slade	75.15.0	due
Skinners Boy Adam	205.0.6	due
Paid Wills & Beasley	2.0.0	
Cost P'd. by Richd Hoskins	5.17.6	
Cr		
By payments made by Wiggins	£602.1.8	
£1043:17 Amt. Int.		

Rec'd the within Order in full of Baker Wiggins this 20 April 1805
Richard Howard

For Richard Hoskins the same I gave my note for 3 off to Howard which the Sd. R. Hoskins owes me now for the [?]

Mr Baker Wiggins Sir, Please to Pay Richard Howard Twenty Dollars and this my Order shall be your Receipt for the same April 16th 1805
Lewis Savoy

                Mr. Richard Hoskins
                Chowan Febry. 1805

Feby. 5th 1805
Dear Cousin,
       The [Torn] has Prevented My not Sending down Sooner, but am in hopes it will Make no Difference, as the weather is been so bad that you Could not of Traveled, I did not get home in 12 days after I left your house, I Was Prevented by the River, We Never had such a Frisk Since My Father Can remember but one, and there never Was One Half of the Propperty lost before, the Old Man lost about Six Hundred Dolls. Worth of Property, I have Sent down the Money to Pay for the Girl that we bought for ready money, you Will Please goe to Mr. Norfleet[?] & Pay him the Money & Take up the small Note I gave him for One Hundred & thirteen Pounds -

Chowan County
Miscellaneous Records

the Balance of the Money you will Buy another Negro, If there is Money Enough you Will Try & Buy Timothy Thompsons Boy, I have Concluded To Take that boy of William Roberts that was Branded, if his hand is got nearly Well, you will be so good as to get him & Bring him up with the rest, If you have Purchased any, I have not sent down as Much Money as I Expected, as Doctr Baker had not sold his Produce, and with all I was rather fearfull, as there is a grate quantity of French Negroes at the Southerd
I Am Yours,
Willis Wiggins

Hamelton, NC
11th Decr. 1805

Mr. Richard Hoskins
Care of Mr. Ed. Hoskins
Edenton

Dear Richard,
    I am a little Surprised that I never have Rec'd a letter from you, respecting Our business, I wanted to offten to Know whether Mr. Norfleet has Ever brought Suit against you & Cousin Baker for them Negroes, the Negro boy Limus I have not Sold, Nor I don't Suppose Shall Shortly as I am afraid he is got the Dropsy or Some Other bad Complaint, he is in a Verry bad Situation.
    Brother Baker has Sold your lands at the Southard and has made a great Sale, Provided the payments had of been Sooner but am afraid the payts Will not answer your purpose Verry Well, as the first Payment is not untill the 1st January 1807, then the Man is to pay $500 he Sold the Land for $2000 payable at 4 payments.
    You Must be Certain to Come up the first January and Goe [Faded] With Brother Sam after the Money, and Make a Title to your Land, as it Will be Out of my Power to goe untill Some time in March, you Will Please Give Me an answer by next post.
    My Love to all the Family
I am Yours, Willis Wiggins.

****

Chowan County
Miscellaneous Records

Testimonial to the Character of Slaves
Estate of Francis Valet, 1807

We the subscribers have had a knowledge this many years of Charles & Mary his Wife Belonging to the State of Francis Valet and do certify they have been Faithfull servants and conducted themselves with great propriety and have acted in a Merretorious manner to their Master particularly in his last sickness. Edenton Sept 14th 1807

Henry He[?], John Popelston, [?] Donaldson, Hend. Standin, H: Niel, Saml Tredwell, [?] McDonald, H. King, Edm. Hoskins, John Fontaine, James Wills, Geo Morgan, JW Littlejohn, Martin Norcom, Wm. Rombough, King Luten, Jas Hathaway, B. Elliott, John Dickinson, John Cox, B. Hassell, Myles Omalley, Arthur Jones.

****

Arthur Jones to Charles Whitlock
Deed of Mortgage

Chowan Registers Office,
    I do hereby certify that the Within Deed of Mortgage was recorded in this Office, this 16th day Decr. 1807 in Book C., Page 343 by James Sutton, P.R.

State of North Carolina }
Chowan County   }

    To all to whom these presents shall come Greeting:
Whereas Charles Whitlock Recovered a Judgment in the County Court of Gates, against Irwin Dun for the Sum of Two Hundred and thirty four Pounds 14/8 3/4 with Interest from the 1st March 1799 till paid and also the further Sum of four Pounds 16/2d for Costs of Suit, And Whereas I Arthur Jones of the Town of Edenton, by my letter to the said Charles Whitlock bearing date the 30t^h day of November 1803 appeared to to pay to him the amount of the said Judgment & Costs. One half in Six Months from the date, which Sums of Money, still remain due and unpaid. Now for the Securing the payment whereof I the said Arthur Jones, have Granted

Chowan County
Miscellaneous Records

Bargained Sold, and by these presents do Grant, Bargain and Sell to the said Charles Whitlock his Executors, Admrs. and Assigns One Negro Man named Frank and one Negro Girl named Becky, To have and to Hold the said Slaves Frank and Becky to the said Charles Whitlock his heirs and Assigns Forever, Provided Nevertheless upon condition that if I the said Arthur Jones, my Executors, Administrators or Assigns shall, and do well and Truly pay or cause to be paid to the said Charles Whitlock his Executors Administrators or Assigns the said Sums of Money and Interest on or before the first day of January 1807 then this deed of bargain & Sale, shall cease determine and be utterly void, any thing therein Contained to the Contrary notwithstanding.

In Witness whereof I have to these presents set my hand & Seal this 12th day of June 1806.
Signed Sealed & delivered in presence of
W. Slade
Arthur Jones   (Seal)

State of North Carolina Septr. 12th 1807
The Execution of the above deed by Arthur Jones was this day proved before me by William Slade the Subscribing witness thereto. Therefor let it be registered
Jn. Hall, Ss. CSC

****

John Little & Others to the Governor
Bond, December 1802

State of North Carolina }
Chowan County   }

Know all men by these presents that we John Little, Alexander Millen & Henry Flury, are held & firmly bound unto James Turner Esquire Governor of the State & his Successors in Office in the Sum of two Hundred Pounds Current Money of the said State: To which payment well & Truly to be made we bind our selves jointly & severally, our & Each of our heirs Executors & administrators Firmly by these presents given at Edenton this 18th day of December 1802.

Chowan County
Miscellaneous Records

The Condition of the above obligation is Such that whereas Thomas Bent Master of the Schooner Yeopim, hath imported into this State a Certain Negroe or free person of Colour from the Island of St. Domingo Contrary to the Laws of this State -- Now the Condition of this obligation is such that the above Bounden John Little, Alexander Millen & Henry Flury do well & Truly Answer to the State & this County for the Good Behaviour of the said Negroe or Free Person of Colour, during the time he the said Negroe or free person of Colour shall remain in this State then this obligation to Void else to remain & be in full force & Effect.

Signed & Sealed in the presence of
H. King

John Little	(Seal)
Alexr Millen	(Seal)
Henry Flury	(Seal)

Appendix A
Glossary of Legal Terms

Appendix A

Glossary of Legal Terms

[Definitions of legal terms appearing in transcriptions within this book are derived from *Black's Law Dictionary*. See footnote below.]

Fi Fa (Fiere Facias): A Writ requiring a Sheriff to satisfy a judgment levied from a debtors property.

Et als: Latin Term, meaning "and others."

Guardian: An individual who is legally responsible for a person, or the estate of a child.

Severalty: Individuals who own real or personal property without other persons sharing in the ownership.

Ex Parte: Done for, or on the application of, one party only.

Solicitor: The chief law officer in a governmental body.

Decree: In Equity, a sentence or order of the Court after considering the case.

Guardian ad litem: A special guardian appointed by the Court to represent an infant or unborn person.

Partition: The dividing of lands owned by joint tenants or tenants in common.

Appendix A
Glossary of Legal Terms

Struck Off: In the language of an auctioneer, by the fall of his hammer, property is to be "Struck Off," which signifies the bidder is entitled to property after paying for it.

Bailiwick: A given area over which a Bailiff or Sheriff has authority or jurisdiction.

Determination: A decision given by a Court implying an ending of a controversy or suit.

Vendue: A sale at public Auction, usually made under authority of law by a constable or sheriff.

F.W.C.: Free woman of color: term applied to all persons not part of the white race, including Indians. The term was not used much after the Civil War.

Commissioner: An individual to whom a commission is directed by a government or a court.[3]

---

[3] Henry Campbell Black, M.A., ***Black's Law Dictionary***, 6th ed. (St. Paul, Minn: West Publishing Company, 1990.)

Table of Cases
Civil and Criminal Actions

Table of Cases

Civil and Criminal Actions

Cases

Dom Rex Vs Moses, a Slave
　Felony
　　Chowan County [1757] _____ 2

Dom Rex Vs. Yorkshire, a Slave
　Felony, Stealing
　　Chowan County [No Date] _____ 1

John L. Simons Vs Thomas Simons
　Civil Actions
　　Chowan County [1832] _____ 11

State Vs Anthony Adams
　Misdemeanor
　　Chowan County [1856] _____ 24

State Vs Certain Slaves
　Criminal Actions
　Outlawry
　　Chowan County [1816] _____ 23

Table of Cases
Civil and Criminal Actions

State Vs Sam, a Slave
   Felony, Attempted Murder
   Chowan County [1781] _____ 3

State Vs. Bett, a Slave
   Arson
   Chowan County [1797] _____ 9

State Vs. Jacob, a Slave
   Felony, Murder
   Chowan County [1787] _____ 5

State Vs. Jacob, a Slave
   Felony, Stealing
   Chowan County [1789] _____ 6

State Vs. James, a Slave
   Breaking & Entering
   Chowan County [1790] _____ 7

State Vs. Jim, a Slave
   Felony
   Chowan County [1781] _____ 5

State Vs. John, a Slave
   Attempted Arson
   Chowan County [1797] _____ 8

State Vs. Peter Cain
   Criminal Actions
   Misdemeanor
   Chowan County [1859] _____ 30

State Vs. Richard Wynns
   Criminal Actions
   Misdemeanor
   Chowan County [1856] _____ 26

Index

A

Acrey
  John, 161
Act of Assembly, 24, 44
Adams
  Anthony, 25, 26
  Anthony, a free man, 25
  Anthony, a free man of color, 25
  Anthony, a Sailor, 25
Ainsley
  Asa, 113
Alexander
  Nathaniel, 103
Allen
  Capt. Nathl, 41
  Nathaniel, 6, 8, 47
  Nathl., 6, 8
Alphin
  Abraham, 92
Arnold
  Hezekiah G., 103
Ashley
  Jeremiah, 48
  Miles, 122
  Myles, 126, 141

B

Badham
  J.C.,
  Commissioner, 177
  Jno. C., Esqr., 176
  John, 41
  John C., 177
  Miles, 41
  William, 48, 158
Baines
  Capt. John C., 68
  Geo., 48
  John, 67
  John C., 68, 78
  Joseph, 63
  Lemuel C., 57
  William, 23
  William, JP, 24
Bains
  William, 9, 48
Baker
  Doctr., 193
  Matthew, 73
  Wynns, 105
Bark
  Moses, 54
Barker
  Squire, 4
Barney
  Geo. W., Attorney, 14
Barritz
  William, 7, 8
  Wm., 7
Bartee
  Robert, 78
Bass
  John, 130, 145
  Peyton, 123
Bateman
  Benja., 44
  Benjamin, 56, 104
Beasely
  Docter, 187
Beasley
  Francis, 41, 42
  George, 48
  Jn. B., 5
  John, 41, 60
  John Baptist, 5, 7
  Joseph, 48
  Nathaniel, 96, 97
  Nathaniel J., 60, 66, 84, 86, 112
  NJ, 66
  Robert, 48, 177
Beasly
  Robert, 176
  Robt, 176
  Robt., 175
Bell
  Arch, 4

201

Index

Saml, 4
Ben, a free Negro, 159
Benbury
  Edmund, 88
  Joseph C., 48, 154
  Richard, 40
  Tho, 7
  Thomas, 7, 91
  William, 72, 110
  Wm., 158
Bennet
  William, 4
Bennett
  John, 41
  John B., 48
  William, 4, 48
Bent
  J.R., Shff, 61
  Thomas, 196
  Thomas, Master of the Schooner Yeopim, 196
Bertie
  Eli, 42
  Robert, 48
Betty
  a free Negroe, 7
Binum
  James, 73
Biram
  James, 90
Bissell
  Capt. Thomas, 41
  Nathaniel C., 23
  Nathl., JP, 24
Bixley
  Nathan, 41
Black
  Alexander, 6
  Alexr., 6
  Wm., 41
Blair
  George Junr., 87

Blanchard
  Micajah, 68
Blanchet
  William, 155
Blount
  Ann C., 164
  Capt. Jacob, 41
  Edmund, 8
  Edmund C., 92
  Frederick, 41
  Jacob, 10
  James, CC, 40
  John, 6, 7, 41, 47, 48
  Jos, 5
  Jos., 2
  Joseph, 2, 3, 4, 95
  Joseph, Esquire, 2
  Joseph, Sherrif, 3
  Mr. John, 38
  Thomas M., 87
Bodley
  Joshua, 151
Bogue
  Capt. Thomas, 74, 76, 90
  capt. Thos., 99
  Capt. Thos., 74
  Captain Thomas, 102
  Tho., 74
  Thomas, 74, 76, 77, 81, 89, 90, 99
Bond
  Capt. Jno. M., 64
  Capt. John, 101, 120
  Capt. John M., 64
  Capt. Richard, 45
  Captain John, 101, 107
  Eden, 76
  Edmund, 64, 83, 92

  Edwin, 20
  Geo., 145
  George, 119, 120, 123, 135, 139, 142, 147
  James, 48
  James C., 80
  Jno, 65
  John, 9, 24, 65, 83, 101, 107, 119, 120, 134, 135
  John Junr., 48
  John M., 65
  John, Junr., 46
  Nathaniel, 23, 61
  Nathaniel Junr, 110
  Nathaniel Junr., 117
  Nathl., JP, 24
  Richard, 45
  Saml. T., 116
  William E, 119
  Wm. E., 119
Bondfield
  Chas, 5
Bonfield
  Charles, 5
Bonner
  Abram, 107
  Capt. John, 58, 70, 136
  Capt. Wm. H., 144
  Captain Wm. H, 145
  James, 131, 145
  John, 58, 70, 83, 92, 93, 115, 120, 121, 131, 136, 139, 145, 188
  William, 123
  William H, 144

Index

William H., 144
Wm H, 145
Wm., 123
Wm. H., 145, 146
Bonners
  John, 92
Borritz
  John, 41
  William, 9, 10
Bouge
  Thomas, 106
Bougue
  Thos, 99
Boulton
  Jonathan, 5, 39, 40
Bouner
  John, 83
Boush
  John, 45
Boyce, 90
  Alfred, 47
  Baker, 90
  Henry, 98, 103
  Jacob, 48
  James, 41, 99, 146
  Jas., 188
  John, 44, 71, 90
  Thomas, 98, 103, 104
  Thos, 117
Boyd
  William, 4
  Wm., 4
Bozman
  Joseph, 41, 47
Bratten
  William, 112, 172
  Wm., 101
Bratton
  Wm., 171, 172
Bridges
  Ballard's Bridge, 78

Brink
  Edmd, 81
Brinkley
  Edm, 84
  Edm., 104
  Edmond, 104
  Edmund, 84, 104
  Martin L., 146
  Miles C., 148
  Myles C., 132, 148
Brinn
  James, 74, 82
  John, 48
Briols
  Francis, 44
Brown
  Agnes, a free woman of color., 162
  Agnis, a free woman of color, 162
  B., 34
  Benjamin, 34
Browning
  Thomas, 35
  Thos, 35
Brownrigg
  Richard, 188
  Thomas J., 54
Browrigg
  Thomas, 49
Bruer
  George W., 80
Buchanan
  John, a free man, 161
  John, a yellow man., 161
Buckley
  Moses, 42
Bullock
  Capt. William, 76
  William, 76

Wm., 58
Bunch
  Abner, 48
  America, 69
  Capt., 54
  Capt. Cullen, 62
  Capt. Elisha, 81
  Charles, 99
  Colon, 48
  Cullen, 54, 71, 75
  Edmund, 90
  Elisha, 69, 74, 77, 81, 89, 106
  Fred, 128, 130, 137
  Frederick, 129, 137, 138
  James, 98
  Jesse, 84
  John A., 148
  Joseph, 42, 176, 177
  Lemuel, 69, 141
  Micajah, 24, 48
  Nuby, 124
  Paul, 44, 52, 56, 61, 70, 74, 76, 80, 82, 83, 89, 104
  Rebecca, 176, 177
  William M., 130
  William N, 122
  William N., 118, 130, 134, 139, 140, 142
  Wm N., 118
Burill
  Samuel N., 185
Burk
  Moses, 70
Burke
  Elisha, 148
  Moses, 101
Burket
  Lemuel, 48

Index

Burrus
  Burrus, 98
  Solomon, 93
Bush
  Capt. William, 62, 66
  Capt. Wm., 67
  J.R., Shff, 68, 69, 70, 71, 72, 73, 74, 75, 76, 79, 83, 84, 85, 86, 87, 88, 89
  Ja. R., Shff, 65, 66, 67
  James R., Shff, 78, 81, 82
  Jas. R., Shff, 64
  John, 44, 67, 90, 173
  John, Clk, 73, 74, 76, 77, 78, 79, 80, 81, 83, 84, 85, 86, 89, 106, 107, 108, 109, 110, 111, 172
  John, Shff, 87
  JR, Shff, 77
  Moses, 61
  William, 44, 62, 67, 73, 74, 78, 100
  Wm, 73
  Wm, DShff, 81
  Wm., 44, 53, 59, 67, 72, 76, 88, 105
  Wm., DShff, 64
Butler
  Capt. Samuel, 41
  Saml., 6, 47
  Samuel, 6, 8, 9, 10
Bynum
  Jos. J., 122
  Joseph J, 98

  Joseph J., 126
Byram
  Isaac, Junr., 49
  Isaac, Senr., 49
  Jas., 49
  Joel, 49
Byrum
  Gideon, 116, 117
  Joseph J, 117, 126
  Joseph J., 103, 104, 116, 122, 141

C

Cabarrus
  S., 6
  Stephen, 6, 9, 33, 36
  Stephen, Esqr., 35, 37
Cain
  Peter, 30, 31
  Peter, a free negro, 30
Campbell
  George, 41
  John, 3
Cannon
  Henry, 95, 97
  J.J., 129
  James J, 146
  James J., 95, 122, 129, 138, 146, 149
  Jas, 121
  Jas J., 138, 146
  Jas. J., 138
  Jas. J. Cannon, 121
Capt Pains District, 44
Capt. Cullins District, 44

Capt. Smalls District, 43
Carter
  Thomas M., 55, 63, 173
  Wm, 41
Chambers
  Saml., 71
  Saml. P., 72
  Samuel, 53
Chappel
  Josiah, 100
Chapple
  James, 49
  Josiah, 49
Charlton
  John, 2
  Samuel, 85
  Tho J, 94
  Tho. J., 15
  Thomas J., 15
  Thos J., 107
  Thos. T., 52
Cheshire
  Alexander, 96
Cheshires
  Mrs., 4
Chishers
  John, 41
Chishire
  John, 9
  John C., 9
Churchill
  Capt. E., 139
  Ephraim, 139, 140, 142, 143, 148
  John, 76, 80, 83, 148
  John Junr., 143
Cochrain
  Thomas Junr., 93, 94, 97, 105, 106, 108, 109, 112

204

Index

Thomas, Junr., 107
Cochraine
  Thomas Junr., 118
Cochran
  T., 47
  Thomas, Junr., 52
  Thos., 118
Cochrane
  Thomas Junr., 148
Cockrain
  Thomas Junr., 85, 91
Cockran
  Capt. Thomas, 52
  Thomas, 52, 63, 84
  Thos, 52, 80
Coffield
  Benjamin, 44, 48
  Capt. James, 79
  Capt. Josiah, 57, 58
  Capt. William, 83
  James, 79, 81
  James:, 70
  Jeremiah, 56
  John, 48, 123
  Jon., 174
  Jos., 57
  Josiah, 58, 79, 122, 123, 124
  William, 83, 173
Cogan
  James, 87
Coke
  Geo. H., 145
  George H., 146
Collins
  Josiah, 47
  Josiah, Junr., 41
  Josiah, Senr., 41
  Mr. Josiah, 6

Common Gallows, 6
Cooley
  Mrs. Penelope, 7
Copeland
  Dred, a free man of color, 162
  Elisha, 37
  Henry, a free man of color, 162
  Jos, 145
  Joseph, 123, 142
  Josiah, 49
  Major Josiah, 5
  Thomas Junr., 137
Copland
  Henry, a free man of color, 162
Cox
  John, 194
  Thomas, 47
Craven
  Penelope, Widow, 2
Creecy
  Aug. R., 139, 145
  Augustus, 135, 177
  Augustus R., 140, 176
  Charles, 66
  Fred., 40
  Frederick, 7, 48, 153
  FredK., 153
  Fredr., 7
  J.S., 56
  Joshua S., 56
  Leml., 5, 40
  Lemuel, 5, 40
  Mr. Joshua S., 56
  Nathan, 40, 48
  Robert, 73, 103
  William, 118
  Wm., 118

Cullen
  Jacob, 111
Cullens
  Capt., 43
  Jacob, 43, 49, 59, 78, 90
  Joab, 67
  Josiah, 75
Cullings
  Jacob, 53, 59
Cullins
  Capt, 43
  Capt., 51
  Jacob, 44
  N.L., 146
Cummings
  Mr., 35
Custis
  Polly, 188

D

Dail
  Abner, 120
  William, 90
Davenport
  C.G., 145
  Eph., 118
  Ephraim, 113, 118, 164
  Ephraim B., 103
  William, 145
Davis
  Jesse, 145
Deakings
  Joseph, 41
Deal
  William, 42, 48
Deanes
  Wm. Deanes, DShff, 93
  Wm., DShff, 95
Deans
  Wm., 146

Index

Devenport
  E., 164
Dickinson
  Capt. Samuel, 41
  David, 116
  John, 194
  Samuel, 9, 10
  Samuel, Esquire, 10
Dillard
  Richard, 149
Dolby
  Stephen, 101
Dominick
  Mr., 160
Donalson
  Robt., 42
Dun
  Irwin, 194
Dunston
  Edmund, 152

E

Eason
  Jacob, 65
Edwards
  Wm., 41
Eecleston
  John, 7
Eelbeck
  Henry, 47
  William, 48
Eelbuk
  J.H., 8
Egan
  Alexander, 8
  Robert, 4, 8
  Robt., 5
Eliot
  Myles, 42
Ellet
  Miles, 152
Elliot

Capt. Silas, 61
  Solomon, 50
  Wm., 59
Elliott
  B., 194
  Capt. Jordan D., 64
  Capt. Miles, 74
  Capt. Silas W, 73
  Capt. Willis, 61
  Ephm B., 119
  Ephraim B, 97, 145
  Ephraim B., 96, 119
  Jordan D, 125
  Jordan D., 63, 70, 126
  Miles, 48, 74, 152
  Silas, 61
  Silas W, 73
  Silas W., 73, 83
  Stephen, 69, 70
  W.H., 129, 138
  William H, 129
  William H., 78, 95, 138, 149, 172
  Willis, 61, 66
  Willis J., 87
  Wm. H., 67, 146, 171
Ellis
  Wesley, 145
  Willis, 89
Eshon
  Capt. Samuel, 83
  Saml., 83, 114
  Samuel, 83, 99, 101, 107, 115, 131, 145
Etheridge
  Daniel V., 64, 112
Eure
  Hillary H., 67

Evans
  Benj. L., 143, 148
  Benjamin L., 142
  Capt. Jeremiah, 147
  Captain Jeremiah, 148
  E., 107
  Edwin, 79, 83, 101, 107, 120, 131
  James, 19, 21, 44
  James E., 145, 147
  Jas, 165
  Jas. E., 165
  Jer., 147
  Jeremiah, 122, 124, 130, 134, 139, 140, 142, 143, 144, 148
  John, 49
  Starky B., 146
  Thomas, 97, 105, 106, 108, 148
  Timothy, 54
Everitt
  Wiley, 78
Evins
  Jeremiah, 130
  Thomas, 130

F

Fail
  Edw, 3
  Edward, 3
Fareboult
  Jas. F., 63
Faribault
  Joseph F, 96
  Joseph F., 52, 95, 96
Felton

Index

Cader, 49
Capt. R.R., 89
Capt. Robert R.,
  91, 104, 109,
  115
Captain Robert
  R., 117
John, 43, 49, 189
R R, 137
R.R., 104, 117,
  128, 130, 137
R.R., Esqr., 129
Robert, 110
Robert R., 91, 98,
  102, 103, 104,
  109, 110, 113,
  129, 132, 138
Shadrick, 49
W., 152
William, 153
Wm., 49, 152
Fereboult
  Joseph, 47
Fife
  John, 41, 45, 55
Fillis
  Granny, 13
Fleetwood
  William, 120
Floyd
  J.N., 182, 185
  James N, 184
  James N., 181,
  183
  Jas. N., 134
Flury
  Henry, 23, 47,
  195, 196
  Henry, JP, 24
Folk
  Alfred, a free man
    of color, 162
Fontaine
  John, 194
Forcom

Dr. John, 164
Ford
  William, 48
Foxwell
  Mary, 181
  Mary C., 180,
  181, 182
Furlough
  David, 114

G

G.W.B, Attorney, 17
Gallop
  Capt. Jeremiah,
  41
Gardner
  Henry, 41
Garrett
  Capt. Edward,
  101
  Capt. Everard, 54
  E., 101
  Edward, 101
  Everard, 54
  Everard, as the
    Capt., 54
  Jeremiah, 86
  John H., 148
  Lemuel, 86, 87
Garretts
  Edward, 101
Gaskins
  Dave, 165
  Mrs., 165
  William A., 142,
  144
  Wm A, 145
Gazette Press,
  Edenton, 14, 15
Gilliam
  Jul, 146
  Julian, 138, 145,
  146

Glover
  A J, 134
  A. J., 184
  A.G., 135
  A.J., 134, 135,
    142, 181, 183
  Andrew J., 175
  Capt. AJ, 142
  Captain A.J., 135,
  142
Goaden
  Lewis, 49
Godfrey
  Jos. G., 135, 179
Godwin
  Thomas Junr.,
  163
Gooden
  William, 48
Goodman
  G.T., 35
Goodwin
  Caleb, 171, 172
  Capt Miles, 118
  Capt Myles, 118
  Capt. Ephraim,
    52, 85, 90, 105,
    107, 108
  Capt. Miles, 97,
    106, 108
  Capt. Miles
    Goodwin, 105
  Capt. Myles, 127
  Captain Ephraim,
    91, 94, 106,
    114
  Captain Myles
    Goodwin, 105
  E., 94
  Easther Ann, 172
  Ephraim, 76, 80,
    83, 85, 90, 91,
    93, 94, 106,
    107, 109, 112
  Esther Ann, 171

Index

Exum, 49, 136, 137
  Henry, 107
  John, 63, 127, 134, 145
  Joseph, 49
  Mary, 177
  Miles, 47, 97, 105, 106, 108, 118
  Myles, 105, 122, 124, 127
  Penelope, 171
  Perry, 64
  Richard, 97, 105, 106, 108, 117
  Richd, 117
  Richd., 47
  Sandford E., 85, 106, 171, 172
  Santford E., 80
  W., 178
  William, 42
  Williamson, 123, 127, 134, 177, 178
Gorham
  Hezekiah, 41
  James, 52
Granberry
  James, 10
Granbery
  Capt. James, 41
Gray
  Stevens, 152
Grays
  Mr., 4
Green Hall, 38
Gregory
  Benjamin, 97
  Frederick C., 86, 92, 108, 114
  H., Estate of, 189
  Jno., 19, 22
  John, 19

Mackey, 72
  Nathan, 55, 94
  Thomas, 88, 94
  William, 42
  Wm., 48
Griffen
  Willis, 49
Griffin
  John B., 49
Grime
  William, 94, 95
Grimes
  Capt. William, 95, 96
  William, 79, 85, 95, 96, 97
  Wm., 95
Grist
  Allen, 164
  W., 164
  William, 164
Guire
  Samuel M., 42
Guyer
  John M., 42

H

Hall
  Clement, 41
  Jn, CSC, 195
  John, 179, 183
  John H., 184
  John H., 158, 182, 185, 186
  Wm. W., 145
Halley
  William J., 47
Halsey
  Capt. Lemuel B., 60
  Captn. B., 60
  Colen, 48
  Cullen, 42, 129

Henry, 135
  John, 48
  Leml. B., 63
  Lemuel, 103
  Lemuel P., 158
  Malachea, 48
  Myles, 56, 66, 93
  Samuel, 91
Halsy
  Collen, 130
Hamilton
  Eliza, 188
Hancock
  Wm G, 165
Hankins
  Capt. Thomas, 41
  John G., 52, 85
  Thomas, 9, 10, 47
Hardy
  Rob, 4
  Robert, 4
Harrel
  David, Senr., 52
Harrell
  Elizabeth, 174
  James, 94
  Joseph Henry, 174
  Martin, 120
  William H., 174, 175
  Wm. H., 174
Hartford
  John, Constable, 4
Hassel
  Abraham, 42
Hassell
  Abraham, 48
  B., 194
  Jesse, 48
  Miles, 45
Hathaway
  B., DShff, 69
  B., DShff, 20
  Burton, 41

Index

Capt. George L., 84
Capt. James, 41
George L, 84
George L., 84
James, 34, 35, 47
Jas., 35, 194
Jas., Senr., 35
R.W., DShff, 82
T.V, Clk, 112
T.V., 12, 64, 67, 92, 116
T.V., Clk, 47, 52, 64, 71, 72, 90, 91, 92, 94, 97, 98, 99, 101, 102, 103, 104, 105, 106, 107, 108, 109, 110, 111, 112, 113, 114, 115, 116, 117
T.V., D Clk, 73
T.V., DClk, 73, 74, 75, 76, 77, 78, 79, 80, 81, 83, 84, 85, 86, 87, 89, 106, 107, 108, 109, 110, 111, 172, 173
T.V., DS, 86, 90, 93, 94, 95, 98
T.V., DShff, 12
Thomas V., 161
William B., 86
HathawayT.V., Clk, 93
Haughton
  Capt. Charles, 72
  Captain Charles G, 108
  Charles, 48, 72
  Charles G, 108
  Charles G., 108

Chas. G., 108
Edward, 42, 45, 48
James, 3
Jonathan, 48
Jonathan H., 55
Joseph B., 60, 65
Leml., 56
Lemuel, 56
Mala, Solicitor, 169
Malachi, Atto., 14
Malachi, Attorney, 12, 170
Malachi, Solicitor, 172
Richard, 48
Thomas G., 77
Haughtons
  Capt., 56
Hawks
  Mr S., 30
Hedrick
  Capt. W.S., 138
  William, 135, 146
  William S., 138
  Wm., 145
Henderson
  Carolina, 167
  Caroline, 167
  Jane, 167
Henry
  Justina A, 181
  Justina A., 180, 181, 182, 184
  Justina Adoline, 183
  Richard, 180, 181, 182, 183, 184
  Wills, Clk, 95
Herdle
  Henry, 49
Higgins
  John, 145

Hill
  Mills, 168, 169
  Sarah, 168
Hindsley
  James, 64, 65
Hines
  E.C., Esq., 26
  E.C., Solicitor, 25
Hinesby
  James, 92
Hinesly
  James, 70
Hinten
  Noah, 55
Hix
  William, 49
Hobbs
  H.H., 146
  Henry W., 72, 79
  Moses, 43, 44, 135, 136, 140
  Moses, Constable, 43
  Reuben, 48
Hobs
  Moses, 140
Hohns
  Robert, 39, 40
Holley
  William J., 116
  Wm J., 115
  Wm. J., 174
Hollowell
  Jordan, 141, 143
  Quinton, 141, 143
Hopkins
  Joseph, 164
Hornblow
  John, 10
Horniblow
  John, 47
Hornsblow
  John, 9
Hoskins
  B., 21

Index

Baker, 20, 22, 48,
  191
  Capt., 51
  Edem., Shff, 55
  Edm, Clk, 54, 60,
    65, 105
  Edm., 56, 194
  Edm., Clk, 52, 53,
    56, 58, 59, 61,
    62, 63, 65, 66,
    67, 68, 69, 70,
    96, 97, 103,
    104
  Edmd, 15, 157
  Edmd, Clerk, 14
  Edmd, Clk, 14
  Edmd, JP, 24
  Edmd., 157
  Edmd., Clk, 15
  Edmund, 23, 41
  Edmund, Clerk,
    14, 16, 17, 170
  Edmund, Clk, 171
  James, 9, 153
  John, 42, 48
  Joseph, 72
  Joseph N., 91
  Lemuel, 72
  Mr. Ed., 193
  Mr. Edmund,
    Mercht., 190
  Mr. Richard, 190,
    192, 193
  Richard, 50, 191,
    192
  Richd., 46, 192
  Samuel, 48
  T.S., 97
  T.S., Clk, 120
  T.S., Shff, 96,
    103, 109, 110,
    111, 112, 113,
    114, 115, 116,
    117, 118, 119,
    120, 121, 122,
    123, 124, 125,
    126, 127, 128,
    129, 131, 148,
    162
  T.S.,Shff, 101
  Tho S., Shff, 116
  Thomas, 84, 108
  Thos T, Shff, 104
  Thos, Shff, 105
  William, 2, 3, 5, 7
  William, Estate
    of, 6
  Willm., 2, 5
  Willm., Estate of,
    6
Houghton
  Jas., 3
Howard
  Richard, 192
Howcot
  Nathaniel, 48
Howcott
  Charles R., 79
  Nathaniel, 58
  Nathanl., 44
Howe
  Arthur, 48
Howett
  Richard, 170
Hudgins
  T., 182
  T.W., 181, 183,
    184, 185
  Thomas W., 80
Hudson
  John, 110
  John W, 118
  John W., 98, 103,
    104, 118
  Joseph, 49
  Uriah, 66
Humphries
  David, 41
Humphris
  John, 41
Hurdle
  Capt. Hardy, 56
  Capt. Joseph, 68
  Charles, 97
  Elisha, 67
  Hardy, 56, 90,
    100
  Harmon, 43
  Henry, 43, 80, 85,
    91, 93, 106,
    107, 109
  Joseph, 53, 68,
    100
  Leml., 100
  Lemuel, 81, 89,
    90, 100, 106
  Quenten, 100
  Richard, 100
  Riddick, 100
  Robert, 81
  William, 81, 111
  Wm., 59
Hutton
  George F., 44

I

Iredell
  Thos., 41
Island of St.
  Domingo, 189,
  196

J

Wills, 21
Jackson
  Capt. William, 69
  James, 42
  James, Constable,
    42
  Joseph, 88

210

Index

William, 45, 69, 73, 78
Wm. Junr., 50
James
  Jonathan, 48
Jamison
  Bond, 48
Janson
  C.W., 41
Johnson
  Cha., 4
  Charles E, 57, 109, 117
  Charles E., 57, 117
  Charles, Esqr, 34
  Chas E, 109
  Chas E., 109
  Chas:, 5
  Robert, 126
  Thomas, 41, 185
  William, 185
Johnston
  Charles E., 188
  Samuel, 6
Jones
  Allen, 79
  Arthur, 194, 195
  Cullen, 93, 98
  Fra., 156
  Francis, 41, 156
  Henderson, 83
  Henderson D, 92, 102
  Henderson D., 92, 93, 102
  James, 48, 156
  Jones, 44
  Josiah, 42, 48
  Thomas, 23, 42, 48
  Thos., JP, 24
  W., 156
  William, 18, 48
  Wm, 21
  Wm., 18, 22, 157
  Zachariah, 48
Jordan
  Abram, 155
  Caleb, 49
  Caleb C., 155
  Demsey, 48
  Hance, 48
  Jacob, 44, 49
  John R., 75
  Joseph, 49
  Joseph J., 112
  Josiah, 49
  Richard, 56
  William, 48
June
  a free woman of color, 162
Justena
  Henry, 181

K

Kail
  Isaac, 125, 128, 130
Kale
  Isaac, 144, 145
Kealing
  Robert, 170
Keating
  Robert Junr., 170
Kennedy
  Henry, 41, 42
Kerby
  Isaiah, 87
King
  H., 194, 196
  Henry, 41
  Thomas, 6

L

Lamb
  William, 95, 96
  William G.H., 97
Lane
  William, 89
Lanston
  Captain John, 24
Lasiter
  Allen, 45, 56
  Capt. Allen, 45
Lassiter
  Allen, 56
Laughre
  Charles, 47
Laughree
  Charles, 10, 41
Lawrence
  David, 4, 5
Leary
  Capt. John, 77
  Capt. John H., 77, 88
  Capt. William, 61
  Captain John E., 127
  Cornelias, 3
  Dr. W., 147
  Dr. W. J., 131
  Dr. Wm. J., 147
  Job, 48
  John, 48, 88, 136
  John E, 127
  John E., 126
  John H, 125
  John H., 77, 88, 125
  John S., 136
  Joseph S., 148
  Lemuel, 84
  T.H. Junr., 178
  Thomas, 88

Index

Thomas H. Junr., 176
Thomas J., 132, 143
Thomas T., 139
West, 131, 132
West Junr., 136
West R., 137, 141
William, 141, 144, 148
William J., 145
Wm G., 145
Wm., 120, 145
Wm. G., 53
WR, 141
Leath
  A., 43
  Archibald, 43, 55
Lemuel
  John, 111
Lenox
  Ro, 3
  Robert, 3
Liles
  Geo., 48
  William G., 72
  Wm. G., 71
Little
  Capt. John, 41
  John, 10, 47, 195, 196
Littlejohn
  Capt. William, 41
  Capt. Wm. A., 92
  Captain Wm A., 114
  JW, 194
  Mr. William, 160
  Thomas B., 41
  William, 6, 9, 10
  William A., 92, 103, 108, 114
  Wm., 6, 92, 160
  Wm. A., 114
Long

James, Shff, 16
John, 145
Louther
  D. Junr., 148
  William D, 133
Lowree
  William, 41
Lowther
  Mixon, 125
  Mr. William Lowther, 2
  W.D., 125
  William D, 132
  William D., 125, 133
  William D. Junr., 112
  Wm. D., 133
Luten
  Capt. King, 41
  Frederick, 48
  Henderson, 39, 41
  Henderson, Senr., 40
  James, 2, 156
  Jn., 3
  John, 3, 48
  King, 9, 10, 47, 194
  William, Junr., 3
  Wm., 3
Luton
  King, 9
Lynch
  L.B., 94

M

M Cottor
  John, DShff, 59
Mackey
  Willm., 163
Malbee
  Jonathan, 41

Mally
  Myles O., 47
Mann
  John, 92
Manning
  Joseph, 157
  Th. C., 180
Mardie
  Joseph, 146
Mare
  Capt. John, 41
Mars
  John, 10
Mathias
  Thomas, 44, 48
Mc Cottor
  John, 57
McCotter
  John, DShff, 168
McDonald
  Dn, 37
  Duncan, 37, 161, 162
McDowell
  Capt. D., 97
  Capt. Daniel, 97
  D., 97
  Daniel, 52
McDowells
  Daniel, 51
McGuire
  Capt., 48
  Jno., JP, 24
  John, 23, 48
  Phillip, 48
  Samuel, 48
McKeel
  Capt. Josiah, 88
  Josiah, 88
McNider
  James, 96
  William, 96
Meredet
  Charles, 71
Middleton

Index

Capt., 56
  Mr. Wm., 56
  William, 56
Midleton
  William, 48
Miers
  Thomas, 48
Millen
  Alexander, 47, 195, 196
  Alexr, 196
Miller
  Alexander, 10
  Mason, 39, 40, 48
  Robt., 164
  Thomas, 162
Millin
  Alexr., 41
Ming
  Deliah, 152
  James, 48
  Richard, 42
  William, 44
Miscellany Press, Edenton, 17, 18, 19, 20, 21
Mitchell
  Henry, 147
  John, 48
  John, Junr., 48
  Mitchell, 144
  William, 48
Mixon
  Charles W., 63
Mixson
  Capt. Charles W., 63
  Charles W., 125, 132
Moody
  Capt. Robert, 41
Moore
  Captain Charles, 137

Captain Chas. S., 136
  Charles, 137, 141
  Charles S., 136
  Chas. S., 136, 141
  Edwin M., 103, 111
  J.H., 121
  Jackson H., 121, 137
  Jos., 118
  Joseph, 113, 118
  Robert, 49
  William, 90
  William A., CME, 158
Moran
  Capt. Jos, 139
  Isaac, 126, 127
  Jos, 136, 139
  Jos., 139
  Joseph, 126, 127, 131, 133, 134, 136, 139, 140, 145
Morgan
  Capt. George, 41
  Geo, 194
  George, 47
Muns
  Wm., Junr., 48
Murfree
  Wm., 49
Myers
  Alexander, 138

N

Nail
  John, 41
NC Counties
  Martin, 161
  Perquimans, 21
  Tyrell, 153

NC Towns
  Hamelton, 193
Neil
  H., 190
  Honor, 10
  Honore, 41, 189
Neill
  Honore, 47
  James, 41
Nelson
  Mr. Robert, 2
Newbern
  William, 69
Newborn
  Jeremiah, 76, 84, 87
  William, 42, 49, 87
  Wilson, 48
Newborne
  William, 86
Newby
  Joseph B., 94, 97, 108
Newell
  John W., 148
Newman
  John, 134, 140
Niel
  H., 194
  James, 47
Nixon
  Annanias, 100
  B., 128
  B., DShff, 102
  Bartemious, 100, 129
  Bartimus, 117
  Delight, 88
Nixson
  Delight, 63
  Erasmus, 173
  Erastus, 173
  Mary F., 173
  Thomas M., 173

Index

William, 173
Norcom
  Capt. James, 66
  Capt. Jas., 135
  Capt. William R., 87
  Capt. Wm., 112
  Captain James, 133, 135
  Edm., 42
  Edmond, 40
  Edmund, 48, 148
  Fred, 153
  Frederick, 154
  James, 133, 135
  James Junr., 86, 103, 110, 111
  James, Junr., 64, 65, 103
  Jas., 135
  Jas. Junr., 103
  John, 60
  Joseph, 57, 60, 72, 110, 157, 158
  Martin, 194
  William, 65, 103, 111, 112, 118, 148
  William R., 78, 79, 87
  Wm., 112
Norcoms
  Capt., 48
Norfleet
  Abraham, 48
  Benjn., 41
  Capt. E., 41
  E, 51
  E, CC, 42
  E., 51, 54, 154, 155, 156
  E., CC, 42, 43, 44, 45
  E., CCC, 42
  E., Clk, 56
  E., CS, 51
  Jas., Clk, 45
  Mr., 190, 192, 193
  N., Clk, 50
  Will, 156
Nowell
  John W., 140

O

O.Malley
  Capt. Myles, 41
Omalley
  Myles, 194
Omally
  Myles, 190
Outlaw
  Edward C., 24

P

Padjett
  John, 48
Paine
  Capt., 98
  Capt. John, 93
  Ebenezer, 41
  John, 93
  R.T., 135
Pains
  Capt., 52
Pambrie
  Dominique, 4
Parish
  John, 49
  John, Estate of, 45
  Joseph, 49
  Nathan, 84
Parker
  Capt. Jacob N., 78
  Elisha, 49
  George, 145
  Isaac, 48
  Jacob, 67, 70, 71, 74, 75, 89, 90
  Jacob Junr., 75
  Jacob N, 78
  Jacob, Junr., 75
  Jesse, 69, 74, 82, 89, 145
  John, 65, 68, 93, 114, 121
  Seth, 48
  Seth B, 125
  Seth B., 128, 130
  William, 49
Parkers
  Jacob, 74
Patrol District
  Benburys District, 55
  Capt Benburys District, 103
  Capt Bunch's District, 53
  Captn. Wright's District, 100
  East Side of the Virginia Road, 54
  Green Hall District, 71
  Middle District, 56
  Rockyhock District, 109
  Town of Edenton, 54
  Upper District, 53
Patrol Districts
  Allen Smalls District, 70
  Benburys District, 55
  Bullocks District, 64, 65, 81

Index

Capt Bullocks District, 70, 76
Capt Hoskins District, 50
Capt Simons District, 50
Capt Skinners District, 50, 81
Capt. Paines Dist, 104
Capt. Benburys District, 103
Capt. Benbury's District, 94
Capt. Blount's District, 57
Capt. Haughtons District, 56
Capt. Henry Elliotts District, 67
Capt. Norcoms District, 48
Capt. Paines District, 54
Capt. Skinners District, 87
Capt. Smalls District, 64
Captain Benbury's District, 72
Captain Blount's District, 59
Captain Howcott's District, 78
Captain Howcotts's District, 88
Captain Satterfield's District, 92
Captain Skinners District, 75
Captain Smiths Districts, 83

Captn Benburys District, 68
Captn James Howcotts District, 77
Captn. Benbury's District, 67
Captn. Howcott's District, 88
Captn. Johnsons District, 61
Captn. Satterfields District, 93
Captn. Skinners District, 86
Cowpen Neck District, 123
District below Edenton, 77, 84, 92, 103, 108, 110, 112, 114, 138, 146
District of Edenton, 125
District of Rockahock, 115, 117
Edenton District, 135
Green Hall, 144
Green Hall Dist, 57, 58
Green Hall Dist., 146
Green Hall district, 53
Green Hall District, 53, 58, 72, 79, 83, 101, 102, 107, 115, 120, 125, 127, 128, 130, 131, 134, 135, 145

Green Hall District., 119
Henry Elliotts District, 75
Henry Elliotts District, 62, 73
Johnsons District, 63
Lower District, 91
Lower End of the Middle District, 62
Middle, 47
Middle Dist, 62
Middle District, 52, 76, 80, 83, 85, 91, 94, 105, 106, 112, 118, 128, 130, 132, 134, 139, 143
Middle District in Bear Swamp, 73
Nash District, 58
Neck District, 99
Pains District, 52
Patrol below Edenton, 127, 131, 135, 147
Patrol Below Edenton, 66
Patrol Below Edenton, 148
Patroll below Edenton, 60, 63, 64
Rockahock, 91, 93, 113, 117
Rockahock District, 98, 103, 104, 128, 141
Rockakock, 65

Index

Rockakock District, 61, 68, 89, 90
Rockyhock, 130
Rockyhock District, 122, 126, 131, 136, 138, 141, 142
Sandy Ridge District, 75
Sandy Ridge Road, 63
Sandyridge District, 75
Sound Side below Edenton, 120
Town of Edenton, 52, 59, 60, 79, 80, 85, 87, 95, 96, 133
Upper district, 78
Upper District, 59, 67, 68, 69, 73, 74, 81, 95, 97, 99, 121, 137, 143, 149
Upper District., 129
Upper End of the Middle District, 60
Upper part of the Upper District, 77
Virginia Road, 61, 63, 66, 69, 74
Virginia Road to Chowan River, 71
West Side of the Virginia Road, 52
PAtrol Districts

Capt Cullins District, 50
Patrol Regulations, 46
Paxton Captain Richard, 113
Richard, 113
Richd., 113
Payne Capt. Michal, 41
M., 4
Michael, 3, 6
Michl, 7
Michl., 6, 7, 190
Mickl., 8
Pearce John C., 142
Perkins Robert, 48
Perquimans Line, 63, 69, 74, 82
Perrin Amasa, 59
Perry Allen H., 127, 132
Caleb, 105, 106
Capt. Calep, 47
John, 43, 44, 49, 129, 130
Samuel, Junr., 49
Stack, 89
Starkey, 91
William, 126, 129, 141
Wm., 130
Pettyjohn Job, 48
John, 42, 48
Lemuel M., 60
Phillips G.N., 41
Pierce John, 127, 130

Pointer John, 164
Mr. J., 164
Popelston John, 41, 194
Popleston John, 47
Powell Patrick, 105
Poynter John, 4, 5
Pratt Joseph Z., 135
R.S., 133
Robert S., 133, 134
Thomas, 140
Prevett Lemuel, 65, 68
Price Jeremiah, 48
Privett William, 122
William Junr., 126
Privitt Capt. William, 142
John, 141
Samuel, 52, 93
William, 130
William Junr, 109
William Junr., 52, 91, 93, 94, 97, 105, 106, 107, 108, 126, 130, 134, 139, 140, 142
Wm. Junr., 142
Wm., Senr., 52
Purdie Ivy, 41

Index

R

Rameekee
  Capt. Frederick, 41
Ramsay
  Ann, 185, 186
Ramsey
  Allen, 8, 9, 41
Rascoe
  Henry E., 92
  W D, Shff, 93
  W.D., 70
  W.D., Shff, 70, 72, 73, 74, 81, 83, 84, 85, 86, 87, 88, 102, 108, 110, 115, 173
  WD, Shff, 80, 92, 95, 107, 112, 113, 114
  William, 24
  William D., 85
  Wm D, 75, 78, 82
  Wm D, DShff, 81
  Wm D, Shff, 17, 20, 21, 75, 77, 92, 100, 104
  Wm D., Shff, 18, 71, 78, 93, 102
  Wm. D, Shff, 18
  Wm. D., 70, 72, 81
  Wm. D., Shff, 14, 76, 90, 91, 92, 94, 95, 96, 97, 98, 101, 170
  Wm., Shff, 12
Rawls
  Capt. James, 73
  James, 73
Rea
  Capt. William, 87

James, 91
Samuel, 45, 56
Thomas, 48
William, 21, 80, 87
Wm, 21, 22, 87
Wm., 21, 87
Reddick
  Samuel, 105
Reily
  Edward, 41
  Edwd., 47
Riddick
  W.F., Solicitor, 175
Riggs
  Edward S., 120
Righton
  Capt Stark A., 119
  S.A.W., 118
  Stark A, 120
  Stark A., 120, 126, 127, 133, 135
  Stark A.W., 118
Rivers
  Chowan, 66, 71, 75
Roberts
  Capt. Frederick L., 80
  Capt. James, 76, 80, 83
  Capt. William, 58
  Charles, 43, 50, 55
  Chas, Sheriff, 189
  Fred L., 80
  Frederick L., 80, 92, 108
  Fredk. L., 80
  James, 75, 76, 80, 83, 124
  James L., 124

Jas, 82
Jas., 80
John, 138, 146
John W., 108
Mills, 177
William, 57, 59, 67, 76, 80, 83, 193
William C., 78
William R., 58
Wm., 106
Wm. B., 60
Robertson
  Captain William D., 62
  James, 80, 91, 93, 94, 114
  James Junr., 85, 106, 107, 109
  William D, 63
Robinson
  C.E., 26
  C.E., Dep Shff, 30
  Charles, 29
  Charles E., 26, 29
  Chas, 25, 30
  Chas E, 27
  Chas E., 29
  Chas., 29
Robough
  William, 47
Rodrigue
  A, 189, 190
  A., 189, 190
Rogers
  Matthew, 135
Rombough
  Capt. William, 41
  William, 9, 157
  Wm, 7
  Wm., 7, 157, 194
Roscoe
  W D, Shff, 69
  W.D., Shff, 82
  WD, 69

217

Index

Wm D, 52
Wm D, Shff, 53, 54, 55, 59, 61, 65, 67, 68
Wm D., Shff, 64
Wm. D, Shff, 57, 60
Wm. D., 53
Wm. D., Shff, 52, 54, 55, 56, 63, 66
Wm., Shff, 64
Roscue
  WD, Shff, 52
Ross
  Elisabeth, 155

S

Sanderlin
  Thomas, 41
Sanders
  James, 48
  John, 160
Saterfield
  James, 9
  James:, 41
  John, 129
  Thomas, 41, 42, 47
  William, 9
  Wm., 41, 42, 47
Satterfield
  Alfred, 53
  Henry, 64, 65, 92
  John, 130
  John B, 141
  John B., 136, 137, 141
  Thomas, 10, 76, 98, 109
  Thos, 117
Savage

Abram, a free man of color, 162
  William, 3, 4
Savoy
  Lewis, 191, 192
Sawyer
  M.R., 169
  S.T., 15
  samuel T., 15
  Samuel T., 79
Scott
  Levy, 60, 63
Seaman
  Capt. Thomas, 41
  Thomas, 9, 47
Seawell
  Henry, 24
Shannonhouse
  W.R., 145
Sharod
  Jonathan, 159
Shaw
  William, 7, 8
Simons
  Capt. William, 67
  Eliz., 13
  Jacob, 5
  John, 13, 16, 18, 19, 20
  John L, 15, 17, 18, 19, 20, 21
  John L., 17
  John L., 11, 12, 13, 14, 15, 16, 17, 18, 19, 20, 21
  John, Junr., 48
  John, Senr., 48
  Mr. John, 13
  Reuben, 48
  Tho, 12
  Thomas, 11, 12, 13, 14, 15, 16,

17, 18, 19, 20, 21, 79, 102
  Thos, 18
  Thos., 12
  William, 17, 18, 24, 48
  William H, 16
  William H., 16
  Wm, 21, 22
  Wm., 17
SimonsJohn L., 16
Simpson
  Capt. Martin, 70
  Capt. Samuel, 86
  Captain Martin B., 122
  Dempsey, 168
  Evan, 152
  Exum, 23, 49, 188
  Exum, JP, 24
  H., 128, 130
  Henderson, 54, 62, 64, 71, 74, 82, 111, 112, 128, 148, 171, 172
  John R., 132, 133
  M.B., 123
  Martin, 61, 70
  Martin B, 25, 27, 122
  Martin B., 25, 115, 116, 122, 123, 124, 128, 130
  Richard, 73
  Robert, 168
  Saml., 47, 54, 115, 128, 130
  Samuel, 53, 54, 85, 86, 87, 90, 101, 116, 128, 188
  Sarah, 168
  William, 168

Index

Skeels
  Martin, 41
Skinner
  Capt, 42
  Capt. Leml., 55
  Capt. Lemuel, 55
  Captain, 71
  Hardy, 58
  John, 131
  Joseph B., 58, 59
  Joseph H., 94
  Joshua, 77, 110, 111, 120
  Joshua C., 131
  Josiah, 24
  Lemuel, 79
  Miles, 101
  Richard, 42, 49
  Samuel, 49
  Stephen, 69, 71
  T L, 126
  T., 21
  T.L., 125, 181
  T.L., JP, 182, 183, 184, 185
  W.R., 178
  W.R., Clk, 30
  William John, 160
  William R, Clerk, 29
  William R., 171, 172, 179
  william R., Clerk, 179
  William R., Clerk, 26, 28, 29, 30
  William R., Clk, 133
  Wm , Clk, 128
  Wm R , Clk, 141
  Wm R, Clerk, 28, 29
  Wm R, Clk, 27, 124, 125, 126, 128, 129, 130, 131, 132, 134, 135, 138, 139, 140, 142, 143, 144, 145, 147, 148, 179, 181
  Wm R., 118, 172
  Wm R., Clk, 120, 122, 123, 126, 136, 146, 148, 184
  Wm R., Commissioner, 186
  Wm. R, Clerk, 28
  Wm. R, Clk, 122, 124
  Wm. R., 118
  Wm. R. , Clk, 25
  Wm. R., Clerk, 30
  Wm. R., Clk, 26, 119, 121, 122, 123, 125, 127, 129, 131, 133, 134, 135, 136, 137, 140, 141, 142, 143, 145, 149
  Wm. R., Clerk, 27
  Wm., Clk, 119, 120
Skinners
  Capt., 42, 48, 71
Slade
  E., 161
  E., JP, 161
  Ebenezer, 160
  W., 195
  William, 195
  Wm., 192
Slasves
  Moses, 2
Slave
  Harry, 33
Slaves
  Abraham, 189
  Abram, 23, 24
  Adam, 192
  Alesthia, 168
  Alfred, 158
  Alonzo, 181
  Amey, 172
  Amy, 171
  Andrew, 171, 172
  Augustus, 168
  Becky, 195
  Ben, 188, 192
  Bett, 10, 191
  Bob, 171, 172, 183, 184
  Bryan, 181, 182
  Cannon, 181
  Caroline, 183, 184
  Catoe, 188
  Charles, 168, 194
  Cherry, 174
  Daniel, 174, 188
  Dave, 188
  Davy, 37, 38
  Delsey, 168
  Derry, 35
  Dick, 187
  Dilla, 191
  Dilworth, 23, 24
  Edney, 164
  Eliza, 158
  Elliot, 188
  Emily, 158, 181, 182
  Esther, 177
  Francis, 189
  Frank, 195
  French Negroes at the Southard, 193
  Galvin, 181, 182
  George, 157, 168, 192
  Godfrey, 188
  Granville, 167

Index

Guy, 188
Harry, 34, 36, 37, 170, 171, 188
Henry, 12, 13, 16, 17, 18, 23, 24, 168
Herriot, 188
Hester, 1⁻ 172
Isaac, 171, . . 2, 188
Isabell, 174
Isbel, 168
Ishmael, 4
Jack, 7, 23, 24, 168
Jacob, 6, 7, 23, 24
James, 7, 8, 153
Jaspar, 164
Jenny, 188
Jim, 5, 24, 153, 174, 175, 183, 184, 188
Joe, 4, 174, 175, 185, 186
John, 6, 8, 9, 158, 187
John Grant, 8, 9
Kate, 4, 192
Lewis, 188
Liah, 188
Limbrick, 37
Limus, 193
Lindsy, 191, 192
London, 4
Lucinda, 181, 182
Lucy, 152
Malvina, 185, 186
Maria, 157, 188
Mary, 171, 172, 183, 184, 194
Matilda, 164
Merick, 34
Michel, 167
Mike, 156
Miles, 181, 182

Mills, 164
Milly, 168, 188
Mils, 152
Minerva, 167
Mingo, 2
Moses, 3
Nan, 191, 192
Nancy, 188
Napoleon, 167
Nat, 188
Ned, 188
Pations, 160
Patty, 181, 182
Peter, 23, 24, 189
Phillip, 188
Rachael, 187, 188
Rachel, 154, 169
Randolph, 188
Rose, 165, 187
Roxanna, 181
Roxilla, 181
Sam, 3, 4, 24, 187, 188
Sampson, 24
Sandy, 6, 188
Sary, 152
Selah, 155
Sheppard, 191
Silas, 172
Slaves declared Outlaws, 24
Stephen, 177, 179
Suke, 187
Thamer, 4
Thompson, 23, 24
Tom, 183, 184, 188
Toney, 174
Unruly slaves, 180
Valentine, 184
Volentine, 183
Washington, 188
William, 181, 182, 185

Yorkshire, 2
Slaves Caroline, 167
Small
  A., DShff, 104, 105
  Abraham, 48
  Allen, 54, 62
  Baker, 75
  Benjamin, 48
  Capt. John G., 75
  Capt. Jonah, 69
  Capt. Obed, 53
  Capt. Willis, 82, 89
  David, 44, 70, 79, 83, 102, 139, 188
  Humphry, 53, 58
  John G., 53, 62, 75
  Josiah, 76
  Obed, 53, 76, 79, 102
  Obed., 53
  Reuben, 23, 48
  Reuben, JP, 24
  Richard, 130, 132
  Willis, 82, 89, 101
Smalls
  Capt, 44
  Capt., 43
Smith
  Alfred, 71, 72, 79
  Capt. Charles, 126
  Capt. Henry, 71, 72
  Capt. John, 134
  Captain John, 135
  Charles, 91, 100, 104, 110, 115, 122, 126
  Chas, 89

Index

Elijah, 101, 107,
  135, 145
Henry, 71, 72
Isaac, 125, 128,
  130, 145
James, 49
Jer., 89
Jeremiah, 91
John, 49, 133,
  134, 135
Ro, 4
Rob, 4
Samuel, 41
Thomas, 142,
  145, 147
William, 136, 188
William H., 145
William Junr.,
  110, 113
William L., 91
Wm L., 89
Wm., 145
Wm. L., 113
Smithwick
  Luke, 152
Speight
  Richard Dobbs,
    Governor, 189
Spence
  Alex, 79
  Alexander, 79, 95,
    96
  Capt. Alexander,
    79
Spivey
  Jacob, 89, 90,
    101, 102, 106
  Josiah, 188
Spooner
  John, 41
Spruill
  Jos, 146
  Thomas C., 140
Squire
  Roger, 47

Squires
  Roger, 41
Stallings
  Miles, 49
Standen
  H., 36
  Henderson, 36
  Hendr., 36
Standin
  Capt. Henderson
    J., 60
  H., 33
  Hen'd, 2
  Hend., 194
  Henderson, 24,
    33, 34, 41, 47
  Henderson J., 60
  Hendr., 34
  Lem., 7
  Lemuel, 7, 10
  William H., 121
Standing
  Henderson, 2
States
  Virginia, 159, 189
Sutton
  George, 148
  Ja, 156
  James, 23, 33, 34,
    36, 156
  James, JP, 24
  James, P.R., 194
  James, Regr., 153,
    154, 155
Swamps
  Bear, 73

| T |

Hathaway, 80
Taber
  Charles C., 80
Tanbault
  Joseph F., 87

Taylor
  Deborah, 154
  Nathl., 49
  Thomas, 48
Thatch
  Benjamin, 121
  H.C., 144
  Henry C., 147
Thompson
  James, 2
  John, 185, 186
  Timothy, 193
Thomson
  Thomas W., 42,
    48
Todd
  William H., 125,
    128
Tomson
  Timothy, 41
Topping
  Samuel, 49
Town of Edenton
  Gallows of, 3
Tredwell
  Saml., 36, 37, 194
  Samuel, 37
Trivett
  William Junr.,
    122
Trotsman
  Timothy, 90
Turner
  A.J., 174
  David, P.R., 152
  James Esqr,
    Governor, 195
Twine
  John, 49

| V |

Vail
  Edw., 2

Index

Edward, 2
John, 9
Valet
  Francis, Estate of, 194
  Virginia Road, 44

W

Rascoe, 20
Waff
  Capt. Edw T, 68
  Capt. Thomas, 41, 85
  Edward, 79, 98
  Edward S., 188
  George, 43, 45, 54, 55, 97
  Jos T, 30
  Jos T., 47
  Jos. T., 145
  Thomas, 42, 84, 87, 96
  William, 133, 135
  Wm., 133
Walker
  Emanuel, 173
  Mary B., 173
Walton
  Geo. F., 104
  George, 104
  George F., 59, 67, 105
  Holaday, 48
  Rebeccah, 154
  Sarah, 154
  William, 45
Ward
  Allen, 119
  Andrew, 119, 146
  Capt. Humphrey, 69
  Captain Noah, 106

Captain Trotman H, 125
Captain William W., 141
Daniel, 125, 128, 130, 145
Fredk., 49
Humphrey, 69, 74, 77
James, 41
Jeremiah, 49
John, 49
Josiah, 49
Noah, 68, 74, 77, 88, 89, 90, 99, 106, 122
Righton, 119
Shadrick, 49
Solomon, 41
T.H., 130
TH, 130
Timothy, 68, 74, 77, 90, 100
Townsend E., 143
Trotman H, 125, 130
Trotman H., 123, 124, 128, 130
William, 49
William G., 141, 143
William W., 141
Wm. W., 140
Warren
  Hamelton, 41
  Jas., 133
  Peter M., 138, 145, 146
  Thomas D., 126
  Thos D., 125
  Thos. D., 126
Warrick
  Henry, 41
Warring
  Hambleton, 47

Hamilton, 9
Webb
  John B., 132
  Moses, 45
  Wilson, 48
  Zachariah, 42, 47
Welch
  Abner, 67
  B.F., 129
  Baker F, 111
  Baker F., 78, 95, 111, 129, 171
  Baker H., 59
  Baker Welch, 172
  Capt. Baker F., 95
  Capt. Dossey, 137
  Captain Dossey, 137
  Dossey, 122, 137, 146
  Drew, 122
  Edward, 49
  Isaac, 42, 49
  Jesse, 105
  John, 55
  Miles, 188
  Myles D., 95
  William, 83
  Willis, 44, 53, 73
  Wm., 58
Whedbee
  Capt. Thomas, 78
  Thomas, 78
Whidbee
  Henry, 71
  Thomas, 41
  Thomas C, 60
  Thos. C., 65
Whiping Post, 4, 5
Whipping Post, 7
Whipple
  Mrs., 170
  Mrs. Sarah, 169
  Sarah, 170
White

Index

Althea, 181, 182, 183, 184
Benj., 188
Benjamin, 71, 75
Benjn., 57
C.F., 178
Capt. Benjamin, 57
Capt. Jordan, 143
Capt. Peter, 65
Henry, 181, 182, 183, 184
Humphrey, 90
Isabella M, 178
Isabella M., 177, 179
Jesse, 49
Jordan, 141, 143
Joshua, 49
Noah, 66, 75
P F White, Shff, 28
P F, Shff, 30, 100, 132, 135, 137, 140, 147, 158
P. F., Shff, 27, 138, 143
P.F., 138, 162
P.F.,
  Commissioner, 178
P.F., Shff, 25, 28, 29, 130, 131, 132, 133, 134, 135, 137, 139, 140, 141, 142, 144, 145, 146, 147, 183
Peter, 61, 65
Peter F., 115, 145
PF, Shff, 26, 27, 133, 134, 136, 139, 140, 141, 143, 144, 145, 146, 148, 180

Theophilus, 73
Thomas, 5, 124
Thos, 5, 124
Watson, 145
White P.F., Shff, 149
Whitlock
  Charles, 194, 195
Wiggins
  Baker, 190, 191, 192
  W., 191
  Willis, 190, 191, 193
Wilder
  Captain Francis, 65
  Francis, 48, 65
  John, 48, 57
  Michael, 57, 67
  Miles, 157
  Nathaniel, 48
  Richard, 64, 65, 70
  Thomas, 77
Wilkins
  Eli, free person of color., 160, 161
  George, 48
  Saml., 41
  Tamer, 161
  Tamor, 160
  Will, 40
Wilkinson
  Geo:, 41
  George, 47
  Middleton, 56
  William
    Thos. M., 173
Williams
  Geo. M., DShff, 85
  Geo.M., 114
  Jackson, 48
  John, 41
Williamsom

John, 168
Williamson
  John, 168
Wills
  Capt. Henry, 41
  Henry, 47
  Henry, Clk, 52, 63, 64, 66, 67, 69, 70, 71, 72, 73, 74, 75, 76, 77, 78, 80, 81, 82, 83, 84, 85, 86, 87, 88, 89, 90, 91, 92, 93, 94, 96, 98, 101, 102
  Henry, D Clk, 59
  Henry, DC, 57, 58, 59, 60, 61, 62, 63, 65, 68
  Henry, DClk, 169
Ja
  , Clk, 20
  Ja, Clk, 18, 19, 20, 21
  Ja., Clk, 16, 17, 19
  James, 41, 96, 194
  James, Clerk, 16, 17, 18, 19, 20, 21
Wilson
  James, 125, 128, 130, 145
  Jesse, Attorney, 18
Winborne
  R.H., 146
Winslow
  Cader, 121
  Isard, 69
  Job, 100
  Joseph, 100
  Kedar, 119

223

Index

William H., 137
Wipping Post, 2
Bennett, 96
Skinner, 100
Wood
  Allen, 103
  Edw., 132
  Edward, 132
Woodley
  Charles, 133, 136, 139
  Chas., 145
Woodward
  Edward, 49
  James, 174, 175
  Jno. M., 21
  Maria, 174
  Nathaniel, 145

Nathl Junr., 145
Richard, 49
Wright
  Capt. Myles, 53
  Captn., 100
  Humphry, 52
  Miles, 44, 67, 72, 73, 75, 95, 97, 100
  Mr., 190
  Myles, 45, 53
  Townsend, 86, 103, 180, 181
  Townsend:, 182
  William, 191
  Wm., 37, 38
Writ of Outlawry, 23
Wyate

William, 41
Wyatt
  John, 169, 170
  John B., 171
  Sarah, 170
Wynn
  Benjamin, 67
  J.D., JP, 183
  James D., 181
  James D., JP, 184
  Richard, 29
Wynns
  Benjamin, 94
  Richard, 27, 28, 29
  Richard, of color, 30

About The Author:

William L. Byrd III has been involved in genealogical and historical research for more than thirty years. His primary areas of interest are Native Americans, African Americans, West Indians, East Indians and Moors in Virginia, North Carolina, and South Carolina.

He has been published by the *North Carolina Genealogical Society Journal*, the *Magazine of Virginia Genealogy*, *The Rowan County Register*, and *The South Carolina Magazine of Ancestral Research*. He has also co-authored articles with Sheila Stover in the *North Carolina Genealogical Society Journal*, *The Augustan Society Omnibus*, the *Pan-American Indian Association News*, and the *Eagle: New England's American Indian Journal*. He has received an "**Award of Special Recognition**" from **The North Carolina Society of Historians** in the category of "**The History Article Award**" for preserving North Carolina history.

He is a U.S. Army Veteran from the Vietnam era, and served with the U.S. Armed Forces Overseas. He is currently retired, and resides with his family in Hickory, North Carolina.

Heritage Books by William L. Byrd, III:

Against the Peace and Dignity of the State: North Carolina Laws Regarding Slaves, Free Persons of Color, and Indians

Bladen County, North Carolina Tax Lists: 1768 through 1774, Volume I

Bladen County, North Carolina Tax Lists: 1775 through 1789, Volume II

For So Long as the Sun and Moon Endure: Indian Records from the North Carolina General Assembly Sessions, & Other Sources

In Full Force and Virtue: North Carolina Emancipation Records, 1713–1860

North Carolina General Assembly Sessions Records: Slaves and Free Persons of Color, 1709–1789

North Carolina Slaves and Free Persons of Color: Chowan County, Volume One

North Carolina Slaves and Free Persons of Color: Chowan County, Volume Two

North Carolina Slaves and Free Persons of Color: Pasquotank County

North Carolina Slaves and Free Persons of Color: Perquimans County

Villainy Often Goes Unpunished: Indian Records from the North Carolina General Assembly Sessions, 1675–1789

Heritage Books by William L. Byrd, III and John H. Smith:

North Carolina Slaves and Free Persons of Color: Burke, Lincoln, and Rowan Counties

North Carolina Slaves and Free Persons of Color: Hyde and Beaufort Counties

North Carolina Slaves and Free Persons of Color: Iredell County

North Carolina Slaves and Free Persons of Color: Mecklenburg, Gaston, and Union Counties

North Carolina Slaves and Free Persons of Color: McDowell County

North Carolina Slaves and Free Persons of Color: Stokes and Yadkin Counties

www.ingramcontent.com/pod-product-compliance
Lightning Source LLC
Chambersburg PA
CBHW051047160426
43193CB00010B/1098